George Orwell

Volume Two
No. 2

George Orwell

Publishing Office
Abramis Academic
ASK House
Northgate Avenue
Bury St. Edmunds
Suffolk
IP32 6BB
UK

Tel: +44 (0)1284 700321
Fax: +44 (0)1284 717889
Email: info@abramis.co.uk
Web: www.abramis.co.uk

Copyright
All rights reserved. No part of this publication may be reproduced in any material form (including photocopying or storing it in any medium by electronic means, and whether or not transiently or incidentally to some other use of this publication) without the written permission of the copyright owner, except in accordance with the provisions of the Copyright, Designs and Patents Act 1988, or under terms of a licence issued by the Copyright Licensing Agency Ltd, 33-34, Alfred Place, London WC1E 7DP, UK. Applications for the copyright owner's permission to reproduce part of this publication should be addressed to the Publishers.

© 2018 George Orwell Studies & Abramis Academic

ISSN 2399-1267
ISBN 978-1-84549-727-9

George Orwell

Contents

Editorial
How Orwell has Become a Brand in the Capitalist Marketplace – by Richard Lance Keeble — Page 3

Articles
More Orwellian than Feminist: Comparing *Nineteen Eighty-Four* and Margaret Atwood's *The Handmaid's Tale* – by Ron Bateman — Page 6

Collecting Orwell: A Kind of Compulsion – by Darcy Moore — Page 14

Papers
'This Poor Wailer Among the Rebels': Orwell, O'Casey and Ireland – by John Newsinger — Page 20

'A Strange Desire of Wandering': The Female Body and the Problematic Structure of *A Clergyman's Daughter* – by Zhang Weiliang — Page 39

Nineteen Eighty-Four and *Brave New World*: Complementary Visions Reconsidered – by Anna Vaninskaya — Page 50

'Such, Such Were the Joys' and the Journalistic Imagination – by Richard Lance Keeble — Page 69

Reviews
Michael McCluskey on *Modernism at the Microphone: Radio, Propaganda, and Literary Aesthetics during World War II*, by Melissa Dinsman; Jason Finch on *London Writing of the 1930s*, by Anna Cottrell; and Beci Carver on *Modern Print Artefacts: Textual Materiality and British Literary Value in British Print Culture, 1890s-1930s*, by Patrick Collier — Page 91

Front cover image of George Orwell: courtesy of the Orwell Estate

Editors
John Newsinger — Bath Spa University
Richard Lance Keeble — University of Lincoln

Reviews Editor
Luke Seaber — University College London

Production Editor
Paul Anderson — University of Essex

Editorial Board
Kristin Bluemel — Monmouth University, New Jersey
Tim Crook — Goldsmiths, University of London
Peter Marks — University of Sydney
Marina Remy — Paris Sorbonne
Jean Seaton — University of Westminster
Peter Stansky — Stanford University, US
D. J. Taylor — Author, journalist, biographer of Orwell
Florian Zollmann — Newcastle University

EDITORIAL

How Orwell has Become a Brand in the Capitalist Marketplace

RICHARD LANCE KEEBLE

George Orwell lived just 46 years and was writing only between 1929 and 1949. Yet he remains a constant source of fascination for readers, researchers and students across the globe – and hardly a week goes by without some mention of Orwell (or 'Orwellian') in the media. For instance, recently a three-page letter he wrote while recovering in hospital from tuberculosis was expected to fetch $15,000 at an auction in the United States. Signed 'George', the letter, dated 8 March 1948, was written to the novelist Anthony Powell.

In his article in this edition of *George Orwell Studies*, Darcy Moore, an avid collector of Orwelliana, writes: 'Genuine first editions are extremely rare. It is rare to find any of his books from the thirties listed under £600 and it is more likely you will be requested to part with £1,000 for a flawed copy. In 2010, a signed copy of Orwell's first book, *Down and Out in Paris and London*, with a dust jacket, sold for £101,050 (inclusive of the buyer's premium).' How extraordinary. So Orwell, the socialist, the man who fled the clamour of London to the remote Scottish island of Jura to lead a simple life and complete his masterpiece, *Nineteen Eighty-Four*, has become a brand in the capitalist marketplace!

New insights into Orwell's life and works are constantly appearing and questions about his writing styles and events in his life continue to intrigue. Let us take, for instance, the mystery which has always surrounded Orwell's encounter with the American novelist, Ernest Hemingway, in Paris in March 1945. A recently published biography of Hemingway may provide some new clues (Keeble 2017a).

According to Carlos Baker, author of the first Hemingway biography (1972), the two met at the Paris Ritz where the American was staying while reporting on the closing months of the Second World War. Orwell was also in Paris, staying at the Hotel Scribe, covering the war for the *Observer* and *Manchester Evening News*.

Based on a letter Hemingway wrote to the critic Harvey Breit on 16 April 1952 (so more than two years after Orwell had died), Baker records Orwell saying that he feared the communists were out to kill him – and asked for the loan of a pistol. Hemingway duly gave him a .32 Colt that Paul Willerts had given him. Orwell departed 'like a pale ghost'. The story is repeated in Hemingway's memoir, *True at First Light*, published posthumously in his centennial year, 1999, and in the autobiography, *Dante Called You Beatrice* (1960), by the poet and friend of Orwell, Paul Potts. But in all his writings, Orwell never mentioned the meeting.

Did the meeting ever happen? John Rodden and John Rossi go through all the evidence meticulously – and, in the end, remain doubtful (2009). Both Hemingway and Potts were prone to fabrication: could the story have emerged from the novelist's desire to associate himself with a writer whose fame was beginning to outstrip his own? Was Potts desperate to associate himself with a great man?

But if the encounter did take place, it would fit into Orwell's pattern of behaviour in Paris. Most of the men he met were, in some way, linked to intelligence. Malcolm Muggeridge had been assigned by British intelligence to keep watch on the comic novelist P. G. Wodehouse who was suspected of having Nazi sympathies following his broadcasts in the summer of 1941 from Berlin for the American CBS network. Orwell had written an article in defence of Wodehouse in February just before leaving on his reporting assignment (though it was not published until July in the *Windmill* magazine) and so was probably pleased to be introduced to the creator of Jeeves and Bertie Wooster by Muggeridge.

Orwell also met the philosopher (and fellow old Etonian) A. J. 'Freddie' Ayer, in Paris for the Secret Intelligence Service (MI6) who were particularly concerned about the danger of a communist coup. Most evenings in Paris, Orwell dined with Harold Acton whom he had known vaguely at Eton and who was working as a press censor for SHAEF (the Supreme Headquarters Allied Expeditionary Force), then based at the palace of Versailles.

Perhaps the closest clues to Orwell's possible intelligence links lie in his extremely close friendship with David Astor, the millionaire *Observer* journalist whose father owned the newspaper and who was to be its celebrated editor from 1948 to 1975 (Cockett 1991). Astor's intelligence ties went back as far as 1939 when he did 'secret service stuff', according to his cousin, Joyce Grenfell (Macintyre 2014). He served in the early part of the Second World War in naval intelligence alongside Ian Fleming (later author of the James Bond spy thrillers) and with the covert Special Operations Executive (SOE). Thereafter, he always maintained close links to intelligence.

Was Orwell's war reporting assignment a cover for an intelligence mission of some kind? Dorril, in his seminal history of MI6 (2000), reports that, in 1944, Astor was transferred to a unit liaising between SOE and the resistance in France, helping the French underground in London spread the word to groups throughout Europe. While in Paris, perhaps inspired by Astor, Orwell attended the first conference of the Committee for European Federation, bringing together resistance groups from around Europe. The French novelist and editor of *Combat*, Albert Camus, was amongst those present. Astor was later adamant that Orwell had no intelligence links (Keeble 2017b: 42).

Yet, evidence provided in Nicholas Reynold's new biography of Hemingway (2017) may support the view that his encounter with Orwell was in some way linked to intelligence work. Reynolds suggests that Hemingway was actually first recruited as an agent by Russian intelligence, the NKVD, in 1940. But his ties to the Soviets quickly lapsed and, thereafter, Hemingway worked closely with the American Office of Naval Intelligence in Cuba and then with the Office of Strategic Services (the OSS, forerunner of the CIA) in Europe after D-Day. Always addicted to intrigue, Hemingway, while in Cuba, had created an informal 'counter-intelligence bureau' (which he called the 'Crook Factory') to hunt and report on suspicious characters in Havana and throughout Cuba. In another scheme, Hemingway used his fishing boat, the Pilar, to hunt for German submarines in the Caribbean.

In France, the OSS Operational Groups, to which Hemingway was tied, were concentrating in 1945 on supporting and training resistance groups. Could it have been to discuss these activities that Orwell sought out the American novelist? We will never know.

REFERENCES

Baker, Carlos (1972) *Ernest Hemingway: A Life Story*, Harmondsworth: Penguin

Cockett, Richard (1991) *David Astor and the Observer*, London: Deutsch

Dorril, Stephen (2000) *MI6: Fifty Years of Special Operations*, London: Fourth Estate

Keeble, Richard Lance (2017a) Orwell and Hemingway: The mystery deepens, *orwellsocietyblog*, 17 December. Available online at https://orwellsocietyblog.wordpress.com/2017/12/17/hemingway-and-orwell-1945/

Keeble, Richard Lance (2017b) *Covering Conflict: The Making and Unmaking of New Militarism*, Bury St Edmunds: Abramis

Macintyre, Ben (2014) *A Spy Among Friends: Kim Philby and the Great Betrayal*, London: Bloomsbury

Rodden, John and Rossi, John (2009) The mysterious (un)meeting between George Orwell and Ernest Hemingway, the *Kenyon Review*, Vol. 31, No. 4. Available online at https://www.kenyonreview.org/journal/fall-2009/selections/john-rodden-and-john-rossi/

Reynolds, Nicholas (2017) *Writer, Sailor, Soldier, Spy: Ernest Hemingway's Secret Adventures, 1935-1961*, London: HarperCollins

ARTICLE

More Orwellian than Feminist: Comparing *Nineteen Eighty-Four* and Margaret Atwood's *The Handmaid's Tale*

RON BATEMAN

The television adaptation of Margaret Atwood's 1985 novel The Handmaid's Tale *has been sweeping up awards since it was first aired in April 2017. Here, Ron Bateman compares the novel to the dystopian visions of George Orwell and Yevgeny Zamyatin. And he argues that Atwood's work is not the feminist dystopia that it appears to be: rather the society she has created utilises many similar elements identifiable within Orwell's* Nineteen Eighty-Four.

Despite winning the Arthur C. Clark award for Science Fiction, Atwood insists that *The Handmaid's Tale* is 'speculative' and has little to do with science fiction. 'There are no Martians. No space travel. We have all the technology we need to put the system in place' (Atwood 1998). But now that television has brought the horror of the fictional society of Gilead into the living room, even Atwood herself has found the reality of her novel on the small screen acutely disturbing. Writing of a scene where the Handmaids shame a woman who was gang raped in a process called 'salvaging' she concedes: 'I found this scene horribly upsetting. It was way too much like way too much history' (Cain 2017). Even when you know it is coming, it is hard to witness the central character, Offred, silently being raped by the Commander, while his wife, Serena Joy, holds her arms down. Indeed, what makes the world of Gilead even more realisable is its reliance on women being complicit in its creation.

If that ordeal is unpalatable enough, in the television series the Handmaids also endure clitoridectomies, or have their eyes plucked from their heads as punishment for the milder forms of dissent. We also witness the Handmaids hurrying past lines of bodies hanging from Walls, damned and executed for being either gay, Catholic, or abortion clinic workers – the newer society refers to homosexuality as 'gender treachery' (1985 [1996: 54]). These 'criminals and deviants' are meant to be stared at – they are meant to scare – they are a vital means of maintaining discipline. Offred is unfazed by the sight of the swinging corpses of the doctors and scientists that had been purged. The people of Gilead are supposed to feel hatred and scorn towards them. Offred feels nothing. The abortions they performed were perfectly legal at the time – and now, by preventing births, they have committed atrocities and paid the ultimate price for their crime. Any mention of what went before is outlawed, and memories of life before Gilead are classified as *attacks of the past*.

ORWELL, ZAMYATIN – AND ATWOOD

A work of dystopian fiction is always more likely to capture the reader's attention when the future world that is created, either is, or becomes disturbingly imaginable. George Orwell created such a world at a time when a section of the British intelligentsia had begun to view Stalinist Russia as a better way forward for a war-torn and virtually bankrupt Britain. Orwell borrowed aspects of his plot from the novel, *We* (1924 [1993]), by Russian author Yevgeny Zamyatin. Owing to publication difficulties, for many years *We* was little known; its strangely harmonious atmosphere meant that it never made the same chilling impact as Orwell's dystopia. The bleakness of Orwell's vision sets it apart from most, if not all of the earlier examples of dystopian fiction, and it is that dull-grey 'Orwellian' world of rigid conformity, continuous executions, fake war, and spies that Margaret Atwood successfully managed to emulate in *The Handmaid's Tale*; albeit beneath the iron heel of religious fanaticism.

There is much to underscore Atwood's assertion that her fiction is speculative. One of her key inspirations, she tells us, is her reading of 'speculative fiction' of the 1930s, 40s and 50s 'and my desire to give the form a try. Most of the ones I'd read had been written by men and had male protagonists' (Watson 2017). Atwood states that she wanted to 'flip that and see what such a thing would look like if told from the point of view of a female narrator'. Again, Atwood is clear to steer around the word 'dystopian', even though the 'speculative' fiction of which she refers are in all likelihood the most powerful examples of dystopian fictiuon of that age. Aside from Orwell, one would assume that she is referring to Aldous Huxley's *Brave New World* (1932) and Arthur Koestler's *Darkness at Noon* (1940). To promote the novel as dystopian would be to invite comparisons and illuminate obvious similarities with earlier dystopias – in particular Orwell's. Aside from being anti-utopia, a dystopia imagines a planned dictatorial society with solid red lines between what is legal and what is forbidden – right down to the clothes one is allowed to wear. There are almost always strict rules relating to sexual intercourse – who can have it, how often, under what circumstances and with whom? In dystopias, casual intercourse is typically forbidden (the hedonistic utopia in Huxley's *Brave New World* is the exception here) while pleasure from the act

RON BATEMAN is often eliminated and controlled. Reproduction is separated out from the act and who can reproduce and under what circumstances and with whom are also strictly controlled. The punishments for violating the rules of the planned society are generally brutal and result in death. All of these fundamentally dystopian elements are significantly present in *The Handmaid's Tale*.

There are other similarities to elements of *Nineteen Eighty-Four* in Atwood's novel. Both works cleverly incorporate a narrative that explains to the reader exactly how the planned society functions, incorporating a historical overview of how things got to where they are. Orwell creates a book within a book – *The Theory and Practice of Oligarchical Collectivism* – for just that purpose. In *The Handmaid's Tale*, it finds its way into Moira's testimony, and more broadly into the *Historical Notes* at the back of the book so as not to disrupt the body of the text. Those *Historical Notes* also serve a similar purpose to the appendix outlining *The Principles of Newspeak* at the back end of *Nineteen Eighty-Four*. Their purpose is to inform the reader that neither regime endures indefinitely and ultimately passes into history. Second, there is the illusion of permanent war, the most obvious ruse employed to guarantee loyalty. The continuous war is always going well on so many fronts. Only the victories are shown – never the defeats. It is also reported regularly that an underground espionage ring has been uncovered. Thirdly, Atwood has substituted Orwell's spies for the Eyes, who permanently monitor the Handmaid's behaviour to the extent that the slightest lapse could give her away.

A strict code is demanded and there are so many unknown Eyes that the Handmaids might be interacting with during their daily routine that nothing is worth the risk. Offred is careful not to deviate from what is acceptable conversation and what is not, although there are times when she cannot resist the release that even the slightest subversive act can offer – even if it is only mildly teasing the guardians. Instead of Orwell's two minutes hate, whereby party members emotionally release their inner turmoil and at the same time display their loyalty to the party by ranting at the traitor Goldstein, Atwood's Handmaids are required to attend 'testifying' – where it is far better to make something up than to have nothing to reveal! (1985 [1996: 81]). One could argue that there are also similarities between the novels regarding the dilemma of what (or what not) to believe. In *Nineteen Eighty-Four*, Orwell utilises a concept called doublethink whereby party members are conditioned to accept two contradictory beliefs and internalise both of them. Among the Handmaids nobody knows what to believe. You dare not dis-believe what you are told, and so you believe everything – even contradictory things.

It is also interesting to consider how the regimes in the two novels manipulate the manner in which the act of sexual intercourse should be either performed or eradicated, In this instance, Orwell departs from Zamyatin's dystopian world OneState where marriage and promiscuity are non-existent and sexual encounters are controlled through the issuing of pink tickets or ration cards usable only at specified 'sex hours' (Zamyatin 1924 [1993]) Orwell's outer-party women wear the red sash of the Anti-Sex League and attend seminars on artsem (artificial insemination in oldspeak) and enthuse about the eradication of the orgasm (Orwell 1949 [1983]). In Orwell's Oceania, there can only be one love – love of Big Brother. Similarly in Gilead, arousal and orgasm are no longer thought necessary: they are a symbol of frivolity – something recreational. Sex is not recreational for the Commander either – he is simply doing his duty (ibid: 105). Offred and her kind exist solely for breeding purposes – two-legged wombs is the term best used to describe them. Human love as always is complicated and unpredictable – so it is eradicated. As soon as they are weaned, daughters are conditioned into believing the world is a better place without love. Arranged marriages remove all of the old-world pressure from girls such as cosmetic surgery and weight issues as they are prepared for a life of total subservience to men.

There is also a marked similarity between all three novels regarding how 'fulfilling sexual relationships' have been used as the favoured way of rebuking the regime. In Zamyatin's *We*, the principal character D-503 commits a criminal act in that he falls in love with a certain I-330, a member of an underground resistance movement who succeeds in leading him temporarily into rebellion. Like D-503, Orwell's chief character Winston Smith harbours subversive desires and engages in forbidden sexual encounters with Julia – also of the Outer-Party. Atwood recognises the effectiveness of this form of subversion and seizes on the same theme. Serena Joy becomes exasperated by the Commander's inability to impregnate Offred, and in an effort to 'help' her conceive, arranges for a sexual encounter between Offred and Nick, the chauffeur, which evolves into a lasting sexual relationship. Atwood is open on this point: 'It is pretty much a standard dystopia *Nineteen Eighty-Four* thing, which is that if the regime forbids love affairs, then one of the rebellious things you can do is have one' (Lacroix 1999).

In all three novels illegal contraband is exchanged to reinforce the bond. Orwell's and Zamyatin's plots are identical on this issue. Julia casts off her overalls in *Nineteen Eighty-Four*, just as I-330 casts off her 'yuni' in *We* – both in preference for flowery dresses and make-up. The similarity is maintained in their successfully embezzling contraband by stealth. In *The Handmaid's Tale*, the old world sexy dress is there again – this time given to Offred as a treat by the Commander, and the illegal contraband also emerges in the form of glossy magazines that he also offers to her. He appears to covet an illicit relationship with his Handmaid. We never really discover what the Commander is aiming for or what he is thinking; especially after the Ceremony when he shuts the door quietly and purposefully 'as if both of us are his ailing mother' (p. 106). On the surface, he initially appears to serve the same purpose as O'Brien in Orwell's novel as each central character is taken into their superior's confidence in the belief that he can help them. Whereas Winston is mistakenly drawn into the belief that O'Brien can indoctrinate him into a resistance group known as the Brotherhood, Offred, by contrast, is captivated only by the opportunity to exercise sexual control over her master.

OFFRED – REBEL, VICTIM OR ACCOMPLICE?

The fact that Offred shuns an opportunity to assist Mayday – the underground resistance group in Gilead – can be interpreted as an indication that Offred is not a genuine rebel, rather a passive victim or even a complicit fixture in the regime (Weiss 2009). There is much to be said for this view, for Atwood has clearly chosen not to endow her character with a great deal of revolutionary zeal. One explanation could be that, since this is a novel about power, there are many other power relationships at work – not just power exercised by Commanders or Aunts over Handmaids. We have previously established how Offred exercises sexual and fertility-driven power over the Commander and Serena Joy respectively. Another explanation for Offred's guarded indifference is that dystopias generally reflect a harsh totalitarian environment where it is too late to act and any attempt at resistance is doomed to failure as previous examples of the genre have shown. She repeatedly admonishes herself for her own complacency and rails at the complacency of women in general for allowing things to get to a point whereby they are helpless slaves. Offred may occasionally have committed reckless acts, but is clearly terrified by the possibility of being declared 'unwoman' and of suffering whatever repercussions might follow. Whereas in Orwell's novel, Winston and Julia accept their eventual fate before they are even discovered, Offred is only concerned with staying alive and maintaining her illicit affair with Nick, and shows no inclination to become a martyr for the cause of the resistance movement.

A FEMINIST DYSTOPIA?

In almost every interview Atwood has given since the novel's publication, the question of her work being a feminist dystopia is raised. Considering Offred's position, this line of inquiry is inevitable. However, what distinguishes *The Handmaid's Tale* from *Nineteen Eighty-Four* is its powerful *anti*-feminist elements. There are female protagonists in Gilead, just as there were strong, formidable women in America who aligned themselves directly against the Women's Liberation Movement and succeeded in influencing policy (Jones

2017). Their complicity in the regime is as stark as the complacency of the women over whom they hold the whip hand. Those who seek to classify the novel as a feminist dystopia also fail to recognise that men are equally likely to finish up swinging from the Wall, or being poisoned in the Colonies as the women are. The only men who seem to escape the oppressiveness of the regime are the Commanders themselves – and to a degree the law enforcement organs in the form of the angels and the guardians (a term previously used for the same purpose in *We*). Atwood herself is largely uncommitted in respect of whether her novel should be categorised as feminist: 'It's one of those general terms that can mean a whole bunch of different things' (Watson 2017). In an earlier interview, Atwood is much clearer, indicating that if the story were told from the point of view of a non-dominant-class male, it could still be classified as a dystopia. It just so happens that 'among the things the society controls are women's reproductive capacities. Make up your own mind; read *The Stepford Wives* to get an example of a strict version of the form' (Atwood 1998). *The Stepford Wives* is a popular comparison: the novel, by Ira Levin, was first published in 1972 at the height of the women's liberation movement and it is difficult to define it as anything other than a feminist dystopia. The success of the follow-up 1975 film, directed by Bryan Forbes, established the Stepford Wife as a cutting metaphor or expression of sarcasm – 'a woman enslaved to a patriarchal definition of femininity, a wife who has no life, who is almost literally an automation' (Williams 2007).

We must also ask if Offred's account of her life in Gilead reflects a definitive feminist outlook on her perilous existence. Aside from seeming to be just an ordinary woman caught up in a bad situation owing to events in her past, we reach a point in the novel where we realise that her account has actually been spliced together by men! This is also the point where readers may suspect that, aside from owing a debt to both Orwell and Zamyatin, the use of a centuries-old narrative to relate the Handmaid's recollections in Atwood's novel represents an identical ploy to that utilised by Jack London for his dystopian novel *The Iron Heel* (1907). Only when we reach the final section of the book do we discover that the account of a Handmaid's life in Gilead was something Offred has not actually written down, rather it is taken from a collection of thirty cassette tapes discovered in a recently excavated footlocker hundreds of years later (1985 [1996: 313]). In just the same way, Ernest Everhard's account of his part in the Second Revolt in *The Iron Heel* is only brought to life from newly discovered documents seven centuries later.

A WARNING TO WOMEN?

Nineteen Eighty-Four was written, not as a prediction, but as a warning against all forms of total power. As uncomfortably realisable as her novel might now seem, Atwood is quick to point out that *The Handmaid's Tale* is not a prediction either (Watson 2017). It is also a warning against abuses of power and, whether or not it was her intention, it serves to caution conservative women against colluding with a patriarchy that seeks to expand its power over women. In this sense, some people might argue the case that it is a feminist dystopia. Yet a society such as Gilead could not arise and endure without the enthusiastic backing of women. When the ground-rules for the new society were being laid-down, the Aunts in their turn also became complicit in the regime – they were offered power over other women and seized upon it. They remind us of the *kapos*, those concentration-camp inmates employed by the Nazis to supervise forced labour. It is also worth making the point that Atwood offers very little comfort for women of a future age following on from the fall of Gilead. Even though the regime does not endure indefinitely, there is no indication within the novel's *Historical Notes* that the misogyny has died-out along with it.

In January 2017, *The New York Times* printed the headline 'President Trump's War on Women Begins', outlining a series of pro-life policies aimed at barring aid from going to groups that even so much as discuss abortion. In the following month *The Handmaid's Tale* overtook George Orwell's *Nineteen Eighty-Four* on the Amazon best-seller list – an indication that in Trump's America, Atwood's dystopia suddenly matters more than it ever did in the past. By the time *The Handmaid's Tale* TV adaptation had won its string of Golden Globes, Donald Trump had become the first sitting president to address directly an anti-abortion rally. Having already committed to appointing justices who want to change the 1973 Roe v. Wade landmark court ruling affirming abortion rights, it will appear to many American women that control over their own bodies is again coming under threat.

With this foreboding scenario in mind, it is interesting that Margaret Atwood appears to make a perfect cameo appearance in the TV series. She plays an Aunt and slaps the side of Offred's head during her re-education as if she is imploring her central character to wake up and pay attention to what is happening under her own nose!'

REFERENCES

Atwood, M. (1998) *The Handmaid's Tale: A Feminist Dystopia?* Open Edition Books pp 17-30. Available online at http://books.openedition.org/pur/30511?lang=en

Atwood. M. (1985 [1996]) *The Handmaid's Tale*, Toronto: McClelland & Stewart; London: Vintage, Random House

Cain, S. (2017) *The Handmaid's Tale* on TV: Too disturbing even for Margaret Atwood, *Guardian*, 25 May. Available online at https://www.theguardian.com/tv-and-radio/2017/may/25/the-handmaids-tale-on-tv-too-disturbing-even-for-margaret-atwood

Hauser, C. (2017) *A Handmaid's Tale* of protest, *New York Times*, 30 June. Available online at https://www.nytimes.com/2017/06/30/us/handmaids-protests-abortion.html

Jones, S. (2017) *The Handmaid's Tale* is a warning to conservative women, *New Republic Magazine*, 20 April. Available online at https://newrepublic.com/article/141674/handmaids-tale-hulu-warning-conservative-women

Lecroix, J. M. (1999) *Roman Protéen: Round Table with Margaret Atwood*, Rouen: University of Rouen

London, J. (1907) *The Iron Heel*. Available online at http://www.gutenberg.org/ebooks/1164

Mead, R. (2017) Margaret Atwood: The prophet of dystopia, *The New Yorker*, April. Available online at https://www.newyorker.com/magazine/2017/04/17/margaret-atwood-the-prophet-of-dystopia

Orwell, G. (1949 [1983]) *Nineteen Eighty-Four*, London: Secker & Warburg; *The Penguin Complete Novels of George Orwell*, Harmondsworth, Middlesex: Penguin

Watson, E. (2017) An interview with Margaret Atwood, *Entertainment Weekly*, 14 July. Available online at http://ew.com/books/2017/07/14/emma-watson-interviews-margaret-atwood-handmaids-tale/

Weiss, A. (2009) Offred's complicity and the dystopian tradition in Margaret Atwood's *The Handmaid's Tale*, *Studies in Canadian Literature*, Vol. 34, No. 1. Available online at https://journals.lib.unb.ca/index.php/scl/article/view/12383/13254

Williams, A. (2007) *The Stepford Wives:* What's a living doll to do in a postfeminist world, Brabon, B. A. and Genz, S. (eds) *Postfeminist Gothic: Critical Interventions in Contemporary Culture*, London: Palgrave Macmillan pp 85-98

Zamyatin, Y. (1924 [1993]) *We*, New York: E.P Dutton Inc; London: Penguin

NOTE ON THE CONTRIBUTOR

Ron Bateman is a founder member of the Orwell Society. He was appointed honourable secretary during the society's formative years before taking on the editorship of the society's *Journal* from 2011 until 2016. He has since relocated to Paciano, Italy.

ARTICLE

Collecting Orwell: A Kind of Compulsion

DARCY MOORE

There are few 20th century writers as collectable as George Orwell. Rare book auctions regularly fetch extraordinary prices, especially for his works published in the 1930s. Even secondhand bookshops have a paucity of battered paperbacks on display. Orwell sells and readers hold on to their copies. Darcy Moore reflects on what he has learnt about finding first editions, translations and books of interest for the Orwell enthusiast, scholar or dilettante.

> 'Book collecting is an obsession, an occupation, a disease, an addiction, a fascination, an absurdity, a fate. It is not a hobby. Those who do it must do it. Those who do not do it, think of it as a cousin of stamp collecting, a sister of the trophy cabinet, bastard of a sound bank account and a weak mind.'
>
> **Jeanette Winterson (2013)**

From seven years of age, I collected books. The sensation of seeing them lined-up on the shelf, in order, was deeply rewarding to my young mind. Knowing you could delve into the worlds they contained, at any time, even more so. Coming from a humble home, each birthday or Christmas presented my main opportunity to add to my collection and I certainly preferred books to Easter Eggs. I never, not once, thought of it as collecting. I needed to have the books to read and re-read. It was my library.

My first Orwell was a battered copy of *Down and Out in Paris and London* found in a secondhand bookstore for a dollar when I started university. It is still on my shelf. *Decline of the English Murder and Other Essays*, *Homage to Catalonia* and a favourite, *Inside the Whale*, have been with me from this time at university too. I had been enamoured with *Animal Farm* and *Nineteen Eighty-Four* at school and bought my own copies for re-reading. Over the years, I steadily added to my library, increasingly buying books inexpensively online. In more recent years, I have relished the procurement of quality first editions, often from far afield, some in much sought-after dust jackets. At first, I purchased books I had not read and am not exactly certain at what point in time this motivation changed and genuine collecting began. Now, I have many different editions of the same book, sometimes, in languages I cannot read. Winterson may have a point.

Orwell, besides being an author and avid reader, was a working journalist, essayist and book reviewer. His output was extraordinary by any measure and this provides the collector with incredible scope. Journals, like *The Adelphi, Horizon, Partisan Review* and *World Review*, are particularly interesting as one can see what else was being published alongside his essays, poetry and reviews. Finding a copy of 'A Hanging' by E. A. Blair, in a well-worn 1931 edition of *The Adelphi*, was particularly special. Orwell's opinion of contemporary novels, poetry and nonfiction is enhanced by collecting and reading the books he reviewed too. Lesser-known, if not exactly esoteric texts include the prefaces he wrote to anthologies and novels, including for his literary hero, Jack London. Orwell – obsessive collector of pamphlets – edited *British Pamphleteers Vol. 1: From the 16th Century the 18th Century.* My bookshelves also include translations of Orwell's fiction and nonfiction in French, German, Chinese, Hungarian and Danish, many of them first editions.

Orwell fantasised – when he was a teenager and dreaming of being a FAMOUS AUTHOR – about having 'uniform editions' of his books in dark blue jackets, He never managed to get that desired colour but was, in the last years of his life, focused on having the works he wished to remain in print standardised. *Burmese Days* and *Coming Up for Air* were published in this uniform edition while he lived but it took until 1959 for *The Road to Wigan Pier* to appear. There is nothing particularly uniform about the appearance of the books and a number of challenges often prevented the text being reprinted as Orwell wished. One imagines that *The Complete Works of George Orwell*, the twenty-volume collection edited by Peter Davison that includes Orwell's standard published library and eleven chronological volumes of nonfiction with a further supplementary book of lost works published a decade later, would have met with Orwell's approval. They look great on the shelf.

COLLECTING FIRST EDITIONS
Recent auctions at Sotheby's suggest George Orwell will continue to be an extraordinarily important writer to collectors of first editions for the foreseeable future. A genuine first edition is the first printing of a book anywhere. For example, *Down and Out in Paris and London* was first printed in the UK by Victor Gollancz, in January 1933. A second, and then a third impression followed in the same month. Technically, all three of these print runs are first editions but collectors will value the first impression much more highly. In June of the same year, Harper and Brothers published the first American edition of this book. It is interesting to note that *Burmese Days* was the only one of Orwell's books to be published

DARCY MOORE

in the USA first. Orwell's publisher in the UK was concerned over potential legal action and it seemed safer to test the waters with an American distributor. This novel is unique in having 'Copyright, 1934, Eric Blair' rather than the expected pseudonym. As such, it is a genuine first edition of considerable interest to collectors.

The avid collector may have a number of first editions of the same book. There is the first edition published in a particular country, including translations. There is also the first paperback edition. When a different publisher gains the rights to the book, there is a new opportunity to have a first edition. There may be a first illustrated edition or other printings that are of interest, for example, early editions in Braille. A samizdat edition is one illegally printed, usually in an Eastern European country pre-1989. These editions were produced in unknown numbers using a variety of methods: mimeograph, carbon copies from typescripts or, in later years, photocopiers. There are some unique illustrations to be found in these samizdat editions, including comic versions, especially of *Animal Farm*. For example, I am currently negotiating a price on a Hungarian samizdat, *Allati Gazdasag* (*Animal Economy*). It has uncredited original illustrations on most pages. Collecting always leads to learning and I now have a reasonable idea about the history of samizdat publishing generally, and in relation to Orwell.

The general reading public know that a bibliography is the list of works referenced by an author while writing their book. Collectors have a different definition. Orwell's best bibliographer, Gillian Fenwick, provides an invaluable guide to understanding Orwell's publishing history. Her *George Orwell: A Bibliography* (1998) is essential for discovering all kinds of important and esoteric facts about the author's printed output. One wonders how the American publisher managed to misprint the title of Orwell's second novel. *The* rather than *A Clergyman's Daughter* must have made more sense to them or maybe it was simply a typographical error. Either way, it seems incredibly careless. Orwell's childhood ambition to have a uniform edition of his works grew more urgent in the last few years of his life. One can see why – with such errors from his publishers. Unfortunately, this uniform edition also suffered problems that were only really corrected when Peter Davison's project to publish Orwell's *Complete Works* resulted in his books being published as intended.

Dust jackets are important to collectors and add immensely to the value of first editions. My understanding is that dust jackets were often abandoned by owners and that libraries routinely removed them. During World War Two the jackets were considered to make the books more flammable and endangered the entire collection held by any institution during bombing raids. There are online businesses that sell facsimile dust jackets. This is particularly useful for the collector who cannot afford the high prices requested for first editions with dust jackets. All of my first editions have facsimile or genuine dust jackets except *Down and Out in London and Paris*. My UK first edition of *Burmese Days* has a photocopy made by a very generous bookseller. One can only imagine that taking this dust jacket off a book, on the market for almost £33,000, to photocopy at the library, was one of a calm and very generous soul who understood the nature and needs of the bibliophile. If you have money to invest in first editions, I recommend West Hull Rare Books for all your Orwell needs.

FINDING GOOD BOOKSELLERS

For decades, scanning the shelves for anything about or by Orwell every time I was in a secondhand bookshop has been my habit. It is rare to find much. A quick search online confirms little is readily available 'used' in Australia. You are unlikely to find any first editions at all. I have discovered many treasures over the years, though, most recently an immaculate first Penguin paperback edition of *A Clergyman's Daughter* for $5.00 at a book sale in the Masonic Hall, a kilometre from my front door, in Kiama, New South Wales, Australia. There are several very useful strategies for finding books at affordable, often bargain prices that will assist the collector endeavouring to add to their collection. Luck certainly plays a part, too. Dennis Glover, author of *The Last Man in Europe* (2017) – a novel about Orwell writing *Nineteen Eighty-Four* on a remote Scottish island – gave me the tip that a bookseller in Melbourne had purchased a number of interesting books about Orwell from a deceased estate. It was a goldmine.

Many individual bookshop owners have websites with the provision to create a list of 'wants' or 'alerts'. This results in an automatically generated email being sent when the book you are after is catalogued at their site. AbeBooks lets the buyer create 'wants' that are very specific. You can search for particular editions, price ranges and even for signed copies using their system. The Antiquarian Booksellers' Association of America provides an excellent, automated alert service that recently led to me buying a very expensive first edition for about 15 per cent of the price usually charged. The key is responding quickly once the book is listed online. Professional booksellers will hold the book for you. An email received this year is a good case in point: 'The book was only catalogued today. You got pretty lucky, as three other people have shown interest in it (you were the first so you had first call on it).' Lurking at the Bibliophile and other mailing lists is a good source of information about books and booksellers too.

If you go to bookfinder.com and search for 'George Orwell', 'first edition' between '1933-39' it quickly becomes evident that there are very few copies of his early books for this period available, at

DARCY MOORE

any price. Genuine first editions are extremely rare. It is rare to find any of these books from the thirties listed under £600 and it is more likely you will be requested to part with £1,000 for a flawed copy. In 2010, a signed copy of Orwell's first book, *Down and Out in Paris and London*, with a dust jacket, sold for £101,050 (inclusive of the buyer's premium). Newspaper reports at the time said it had been 27 years since an edition with a dust jacket had appeared on the market. It certainly was nowhere near that price, as listed just six years earlier by Quill and Brush, in *George Orwell: First Edition and Price Guide* (2004), which suggested the upper end to be about 10 per cent of that.

These prices are rarely fixed. Often the dealer has purchased the book for much less than advertised, especially if they have had the copy for some time. Contacting the bookseller, especially if there is more than one book you are after, and asking for their best price, often pays dividends. It is not unusual to receive 20 per cent discount immediately. I have certainly purchased books at half the price requested, especially when patient. There are many booksellers who do not have 'bricks and mortar' stores and, although highly professional, do it more as a hobby. Often they like chatting about books. One example of having a bit of luck with a book I really coveted was with *Inside the Whale*, which only had 1,000-copies printed (and some of those were destroyed during the Blitz). I procured one from an elderly collector in South Africa selling his library. He also sold me a doubleplusgood copy of Orwell's, *Homage to Catalonia* at well-below market-price. Since then I have bought many other first editions from him that were not Orwell-related, as he clears his shelves.

Fittingly, the most recent Orwell I purchased was a first edition of *Down and Out in Paris and London* in surprisingly good condition. It certainly cost more than the $1.25 I paid in 1987 for his (and my) first book. I value them equally. My collection is quite complete with all first editions of the books first published – both in the USA and UK – during Orwell's lifetime on the shelf. I am particularly pleased to have *The Lion and the Unicorn: Socialism and the English Genius* and *Critical Essays* with very good, original covers. Many of my later American first editions have very good to fine original dust jackets. I really only have the very rare pamphlet, *James Burnham and the Managerial Revolution* (1946) along with *Talking to India* (1943) and *Betrayal of the Left* (1941) which I had 'printed on demand' in India, to collect as first editions.

REFERENCES

Basbanes, Nicholas (2012) *A Gentle Madness: Bibliophiles, Bibliomanes, and the Eternal Passion for Books*, Fine Books Press, Kindle Edition

Blair, E. A. (1931) 'A Hanging', *The Adelphi*, Vol. 2, No. 5, August

Fenwick, Gillian (1998) *George Orwell: A Bibliography*, New Castle, Delaware and London: Oak Knoll Press & St. Paul's Bibliographies

Glover, Dennis (2017) *The Last Man in Europe*, Melbourne: Black Inc.

Gollancz, Victor and Laski, Harold (1941) *Betrayal of the Left: An Examination & Refutation of Communist Policy from October 1939 to January 1941: with Suggestions for an Alternative and an Epilogue on Political Morality*, Left Book Club (print on demand book)

Meyers, Jeffrey and Meyers, Valerie (1977) *George Orwell: An Annotated Bibliography of Criticism*, New York: Garland

Orwell, George and Reynolds, Reginald (1948) *British Pamphleteers, Vol. 1: From the 16th Century the 18th Century*, London: Allan Wingate

Quill and Brush (2004) *George Orwell – First Edition and Price Guide*, Quill and Brush

Telegraph.co.uk (2010) Rare signed first edition of George Orwell work sold for £86,000. Available online at https://www.telegraph.co.uk/culture/books/booknews/7519576/Rare-signed-first-edition-of-George-Orwell-work-sold-for-86000.html, accessed on 25 March 2018

Winterson, Jeanette (2013) *Art Objects: Essays on Ecstasy and Effrontery*, New York: Knopf Doubleday Publishing Group

NOTE ON THE CONTRIBUTOR

Darcy Moore is a deputy principal at a secondary school in New South Wales. He has taught English and History and worked as an academic in post-graduate teacher education at the University of Wollongong. His interest in Orwell began at school, thirty-five years ago, when he was enamoured by *Animal Farm* and *Nineteen Eighty-four*. He is currently researching diaries (1876-1905) written by a sub-deputy opium agent who worked with Orwell's father, Richard Blair, in Bengal and intends to publish insights into this period. He is also working on a book about Orwell for a general readership. He blogs at darcymoore.net and his Twitter handle is @Darcy1968. His Orwell collection can be accessed here: darcymoore.net/orwell-collection/.

PAPER

'This Poor Wailer Among the Rebels': Orwell, O'Casey and Ireland

JOHN NEWSINGER

Although George Orwell never wrote much about Ireland or Irish history and society, he did comment on Irish concerns on a number of occasions and had very strong opinions regarding the Catholic Church. He was very interested in a number of Irish writers, Jonathan Swift, Oscar Wilde, James Joyce, W. B. Yeats and Bernard Shaw and wrote about them extensively. He also clashed with the playwright Sean O'Casey who was still settling accounts with him in 1954. The paper concludes by arguing that Orwell's critical attitude towards nationalist movements and their limitations is particularly relevant when considering his views on Ireland and the Irish.

Keywords: Catholic Church, Joyce, Ireland, Orwell, O'Casey, Wilde, Yeats

Orwell never wrote any extended account of Irish history or society, never made any study of the history of British rule in Ireland. All we have are observations that tended to be made in book reviews. But while he did not show any specific interest in Ireland and the Irish, there were a number of Irish writers who deeply interested and influenced him: most notably Jonathan Swift, Oscar Wilde, James Joyce, W. B. Yeats and Bernard Shaw. And, a book review of his attracted the animosity of Sean O'Casey who devoted a whole chapter, 'Rebel Orwell', of his sixth volume of autobiography, *Sunset and Evening Star*, (1954) to a settling of accounts with that 'poor wailer' Orwell.

IRISH HISTORY

On 18 May 1944, the *Manchester Evening News* published Orwell's review of St. John Ervine's *Parnell* (1940), a sympathetic biography, even though written by an Ulster Unionist. Under Parnell's leadership, the success of the Home Rule movement seemed certain. He had triumphantly overcome a shabby, dishonest attempt to implicate him in the 1882 assassinations of Lord Frederick Cavendish and Thomas Henry Burke in Phoenix Park, Dublin, and in alliance with Prime Minister William Gladstone and the Liberals was near to achieving a Home Rule settlement. Most of the review is spent chronicling Parnell's subsequent downfall and death following the O'Shea divorce scandal. Orwell emphasises 'the cruelty and meanness with which his countrymen treated him', 'the disgusting orgy of hypocrisy, English and Irish' that turned 'the priests against him' and brought him down. The Nationalist movement was 'split into fragments' and 'Home Rule was a lost cause'. Orwell sums up what followed: 'English rule in Ireland lasted another thirty years petering out in a civil war and a treaty which satisfied neither side.' This is, of course, hardly an adequate account, even in summary, of the second Home Rule struggle, Ulster Unionist resistance, the Easter Rising, the rise of Sinn Fein, the Black and Tan War and the Civil War. It certainly shows a lack of any close or serious engagement with Irish history.

Orwell discusses how Parnell, who was 'educated partly in England, spoke with an English accent, and was, of course, Protestant', came to lead the Irish Nationalist movement. Both 'racially and culturally', he had nothing in common with the movement he led, and 'had barely a drop of "native" blood in his veins'. He points out, somewhat tendentiously, that Nationalist movements, 'especially those with a romantic colour to them', are often led by foreigners. At least one reason for this was that 'it is difficult to idealise a country or a people that you know too much about' (*CWGO* 16: 189-190). This was, of course, Orwell writing very much as a journalist, because on another occasion he was to argue the exact opposite with regard to Bernard Shaw. According to Orwell, in a talk he gave on the BBC on 22 January 1943, the reason Shaw was able to satirise English society so effectively was precisely because 'he was an Irishman and able to look at it from the outside'. As for Parnell, Orwell was mystified by the ferocity of his hatred for England and the English which most likely 'sprang from subjective feelings which seem sometimes to have approached insanity'.

Once again, this seems to show a lack of any close engagement with Irish history. Paul Potts, one of Orwell's friends who Orwell acknowledged 'has special knowledge of Eire', was to write of how he 'trembled to think what would have been the result had he written a book about Ireland' such was his level of ignorance (*CWGO* 16: 304; Coppard and Crick 1984: 251). It does not seem unreasonable to suppose though that, if he had attempted such a book, he would have taken steps to remedy this ignorance, grappling with the 1798 rebellion and its bloody suppression, with the horrors of the Great Famine and the British government's responsibility for mass starvation, with the Land War, with the Unionist resistance to Home Rule and the readiness of the Conservative Party to encourage and support both armed rebellion and military mutiny. More particularly, it would have been very interesting to know what Orwell would have made of John Mitchel's *Jail Journal* (1854), one of the nineteenth century's anti-imperialist masterworks.

Orwell returns to a discussion of the Irish struggle for independence in a *New Yorker* review on 19 April 1947 of *Lady Gregory's Journals*, edited by Lennox Robinson (Macmillan 1947). Here, he is once again discussing a Protestant outsider, 'an enlightened aristocrat', who both supported but was at odds with 'the native Irish, whom she loved and championed but by no means resembled'. One cannot help noticing a certain sympathy on Orwell's part here, deriving from his recognition of his own relationship with the British working class. Politically, she was always 'for Ireland against England – even, to some extent, for the Republicans against the Free State government', but at the same time her class background and upbringing pulled her in a different direction. As Orwell points out, she remained a defender of the English public schools and sent her grandson to Harrow. Much to her credit, she was horrified by the activities of the Black and Tans, 'the banditti let loose by the British government in 1919' during what Orwell describes as 'the Terror'. She actually wrote articles condemning the Black and Tans but left them unsigned because she did not want her 'beloved' country house, Coole Park, burned down in reprisal as she hoped to leave it to her grandchildren. Even her hostility to the Black and Tans was coloured by 'class feeling' though, and Orwell notes her hope that the news that some Guards officers, 'gentlemen', as she described them, had been recruited into the force, might lead to an improvement in their conduct (*CWGO* 19: 131-134).

Orwell discusses her crucial involvement with the Abbey Theatre, Dublin, fighting against 'the Puritanism and hypocrisy of the Catholic Irish', mentioning, in particular, the furore over Sean O'Casey's play, *The Plough and the Stars*. When it was first performed in February 1926, 'the audience stormed the stage because members of the Citizen Army were shown carrying their flag into a public house'. Even worse, one of O'Casey's characters, Rosie Redmond, was a prostitute and as everyone knew there were no prostitutes in Catholic Ireland or so it was claimed by some of the protesters![1] O'Casey was later to remark that one of those who made this claim was a well-known in Dublin's brothels! Orwell praises Lady Gregory for the support and encouragement she gave to O'Casey, observing that, without her, 'it is conceivable that O'Casey would never have been heard of'. According to Orwell, she not only led a 'heroic life' but one that was 'probably ... useful' (ibid). High praise, indeed, coming from George Orwell.

One other work is worth considering here: Orwell's review of Katharine Campbell Chorley's important book, *Armies and the Art of Revolution* (1943), which was published in the *Observer*, on 2 January 1944. This book, written from a 'left' angle, according to Orwell, came with a Foreword by B. H. Liddell Hart. Orwell considered worthy of notice two general lessons identified by Chorley: first, that in the modern world a popular insurrection cannot triumph against a modern army that is intact and 'really exerting its strength'. He takes as his example what he misleadingly calls 'the Irish Civil War' where the Irish Republican Army (IRA) 'used guerrilla tactics (assassinations, sudden attacks on unarmed soldiers by men dressed as civilians etc)', tactics 'which could only have been countered by a policy of brutal reprisals'.

For many people the reprisals that the British did unleash in response the IRA campaign, the often murderous activities of the Black and Tans, for example, were quite dreadful enough. But there is no doubt that they were, in fact, comparatively restrained. For a strategy of repression to have defeated Sinn Fein and the IRA, it would have had to be considerably more brutal than anything the British government could contemplate at that time. This was not, as Orwell observes, down to 'any excess of humanity' on the part of either the British government or the British army, but was rather 'because English opinion was largely sympathetic to the Irish and world opinion could not be disregarded'. By way of a contrast, the Japanese army operated under no such restraint and was able to crush resistance in China by wholesale massacre. Orwell was to incorporate this phenomenon into his discussion of the British national character in his *The English People*, written early in 1944, but not published until 1947. Here, support for the underdog became something of an English characteristic so that the 'real weapon' that the IRA used to defeat the British government was 'British public opinion'. There is, of course, some truth in this, but only some. What Orwell leaves out of the equation is the British success in splitting the Republican movement, setting the rival factions against each other and in the process arming the Free State faction to defeat the Republican cause. And, of course, British restraint in suppressing insurgencies was, through the nineteenth and into the twentieth century, much less evident when the insurgents were not white. The brutal suppression of the so-called 'Mau Mau' insurgency in Kenya during the 1950s is powerful testimony to that (*CWGO* 16: 51-52).

More generally, in the second point that Orwell also considered to be of importance, Chorley went on to discuss the politics of the military, or more particularly, of the officer corps. As long as military discipline remained intact, the army, that is the officer corps, would be able to blackmail the government. There had been innumerable examples of this. Indeed, as Chorley points out, 'an army whose officers are drawn from the higher ranks of society can never be trusted to support a "left" government' (ibid). Orwell's own experiences in Spain, where the military had rebelled against the Popular Front government, certainly demonstrated the validity of this point. He was, of course, convinced at this time that a future Labour government out to overthrow capitalism was going to confront the same danger. This raised the question for Orwell of whether an army could be meaningfully democratised and yet still remain militarily effective. He leaves the question hanging. His overall judgement on the book was that, despite some gaps in its argument, it was a 'valuable' contribution and, indeed, it remains so to this day.[2]

NATIONALISM

What of Orwell's attitude to nationalism as such? In the May 1945 first issue of *Polemic,* a magazine that requires more attention than it has so far received, he published his 'Notes on Nationalism'. This typically idiosyncratic discussion from the very beginning distinguishes between nationalism and patriotism. It is worth quoting the difference he identifies:

> By 'patriotism' I mean devotion to a particular place and a particular way of life, which one believes to be the best in the world but has no wish to force upon other people. Patriotism is of its nature defensive, both militarily and culturally. Nationalism, on the other hand, is inseparable from the desire for power. The abiding purpose of every nationalist is to secure more power and more prestige, not for himself but for the nation.

In fact, Orwell complicates matters by referring to 'the nation or some other unit'. As far as he is concerned the category of nationalism embraces any unit into which the individual is prepared 'to sink his own individuality'. He goes on to identify 'Communism, political Catholicism, Zionism, anti-Semitism, Trotskyism and Pacifism' as examples of his 'extended' definition of nationalism. This does, of course, render his discussion of nationalism pretty much useless as far as the actual specific question of nationalism is concerned. Indeed, a more accurate title for the essay might have been 'Notes on Fanaticism' and read with this in mind it is of considerable interest. Nevertheless, he does make a number of observations that are useful as far as nationalism in the conventional sense is concerned.

In Britain, he observes, almost in passing, that the dominant form of nationalism is 'old-fashioned British jingoism'. It would have been interesting to see how he distinguished this from 'patriotism', but instead he chooses not to explore this, focusing instead on what he characterises as the dominant form of nationalism among the British intelligentsia, 'Communism'. Nevertheless, he does go on to point out how the 'nationalist', however defined, can justify the most appalling atrocities when committed in the 'right' cause. The British jingo nationalist, for example, can either justify or at least condone 'the heroes of the Mutiny blowing hundreds of Indians from the guns', or Cromwell's soldiers 'slashing Irishwomen's faces with razors', but will wholeheartedly condemn such actions when committed by others.

He goes on to discuss what he identifies as the three categories of nationalism, 'Positive, Transferred and Negative' although, once again, his discussion extends to Communism, Neo-Toryism, Trotskyism, Pacifism, Class Feeling, Zionism, Colour Feeling, Anti-Semitism[3] and so on. His discussion of 'Positive Nationalism' includes a section on 'Celtic Nationalism', Welsh, Scottish and Irish nationalism, 'alike in their anti-English orientation'. What he sees as the motive force of this Celtic nationalism 'is a belief in the past and future greatness of the Celtic peoples, and it has a strong tinge of racialism'. The Celt is seen as superior to the Saxon, 'simpler, more creative, less vulgar, less snobbish' although beneath the surface 'the usual power-hunger is there'. It also involves a failure to recognise the harsh realities of great power politics whereby Eire owes its independence to 'British protection'. Without the British Empire to protect it, Ireland would have been controlled, perhaps even occupied by the Nazis. And he singles out Sean O'Casey among Irish writers as exemplifying this delusional school of thought.

This is, of course, completely inadequate as a discussion of Irish nationalism. Moreover, Orwell does not discuss nationalist movements struggling against imperialism, nationalism as liberation from colonial rule, not just the Irish struggle earlier in the century, but the bloody struggles being waged against British troops in French Indo-China (Vietnam) and in the Dutch East Indies (Indonesia) at the very time the first issue of *Polemic* came out. There was, of course, also the struggle for Indian independence that was of considerable concern to Orwell, one of his criteria for judging the performance of the Labour government. This dimension of nationalism is left unexplored (*CWGO* 17: 141-155).

Judging from occasional remarks Orwell, as we have seen, seems to have regarded Irish independence as being, in reality, 'sham independence', in the sense that Ireland was wholly dependent on the British to protect it from rival imperialisms. He made a similar point about Indian independence in *The Lion and the Unicorn: Socialism and the English Genius* (1941). As he somewhat brutally put it, 'backward agricultural countries can no more be independent than a cat or a dog'. What he urged, at this time, was the replacement of the British Empire by an alliance of equals between a socialist Britain and its colonies that would be best equipped to confront and defeat Fascism. A socialist Britain would put an end to the exploitation of the colonies once and for all – even if it meant a lower standard of living at home. Instead, it would help with their economic (rather than capitalist) development that benefited 'the Indian coolies'. British protection would, he thought, still remain necessary though 'until such time as the world has ceased to be ruled by bombing planes' (*CWGO* 12: 424-426).

Such an alliance of equals required a socialist revolution in Britain because, quite understandably, no serious nationalist movement would place any trust in the good faith of British political leaders, either Conservative or Labour, given their past record. Even given this, he seems to have regarded Irish neutrality during the fight against the Nazis as a betrayal of sorts. Nevertheless, when Sebastian Haffner, a German exile who collaborated with him and Tosco Fyvel on the Searchlight books project in 1941-1942, argued that the British should forcibly occupy Ireland's ports to protect British shipping, he rejected the idea. According to Haffner, letting 'a sham-independent country like Ireland defy us simply makes all Europe laugh at us'. This was, Orwell thought, a very European way of thinking, whereas neither British nor American public opinion would stand for such a gratuitous violation of neutrality (*CWGO* 12: 444-445), although once again this really only applied to countries where the inhabitants were white.

THE CATHOLIC CHURCH

To what extent was Orwell's attitude towards Ireland and the Irish influenced by his hostility to the Catholic Church? According to Michael Brennan, in his *George Orwell and Religion* (2017), Orwell had a 'habitual predilection for Catholic bashing', 'an ingrained religious bigotry', 'a sneering dislike of Catholicism', and that while his thinking was, on many issues, not static but changed and developed over the years, this was not true with respect to his attitude towards the Catholic Church which 'remained unwaveringly hostile' throughout his life. One likely result of this was Orwell's 'inbuilt antipathy towards small nationalist movements (such as Irish nationalism)'. Brennan's discussion is particularly useful when he looks at *The Road to Wigan Pier* (1937) and its failure to engage with 'Lancashire's Roman Catholics, who at this period sometimes comprised twenty-five per cent or more of the workforce in manual or lower middle-class occupations'. If only Orwell had devoted as much time to say 'a local community of Irish immigrant Catholics in Liverpool as he did to unemployed miners in Wigan and Barnsley' then this would have mitigated his commentary in the second part of *The Road* and 'undermined Orwell's polemical antipathy towards the Catholic hierarchy' (Brennan 2017: xviii, 49, 56, 59, 73).

While this is valid up to a point, and such an inquiry on Orwell's part would certainly have been interesting, it does make the mistake of seeing the first part of *The Road* as some sort of objective sociological enquiry rather than as a work of well-researched propaganda, focusing on mining communities and their plight as the best way to advance the socialist cause. Moreover, it also seems clear that his hostility to Catholicism was not actually sustained by any kind of religious bigotry but rather by the fact that he saw the Catholic Church as *generally* operating as a bastion of reaction, not just in Britain, but on the Continent as well.

As far as Britain was concerned, he discussed the Catholic Church and its adherents in one of his 'London Letters' to *Partisan Review*, published in the November-December 1941 issue. Here he considered Catholic attitudes. There were, he wrote, 'some two million Catholics in the country, the bulk of them very poor Irish labourers. They vote Labour and act as a sort of silent drag on Labour Party policy'. Working class Catholics were not enough under the thumb of their parish priests 'to be Fascist in sympathy', but as far as middle and upper class Catholics were concerned, 'I suppose I need not repeat the history of their pro-Fascist activities'. Their wartime sympathies were with Franco and Pétain rather than with the Nazis although he thought they would support 'any plausible terms … for a compromise peace'. Indeed, he concluded, these people 'are the only really conscious, logical, intelligent enemies that democracy has got in England, and it is a mistake to despise them' (*CWGO* 13: 548-549).

His criticism of the Catholic Church in Spain was that it was 'part of the status quo' with 'its influence on the side of the wealthy'. As far as many of 'the Spanish common people' were concerned, the Catholic Church was 'simply a racket and the priest, the boss and the landlord were all of a piece'. It was this that accounted for the ferocity of popular anti-clericalism (*CWGO* 11: 234). But this was not all he had to say. Indeed, when he came to review Jose Antonio de Aguirre's memoir, *Freedom Was Flesh and Blood*, in July 1945, he displayed a remarkable absence of religious bigotry. Aguirre was the former President of the Basque Republic, who had fled from Spain, along with 'about 200,000' other Basques, overwhelmingly Catholics, after Franco's victory. Orwell describes the book as 'valuable because it expresses the outlook of a Catholic democrat' and actually laments the fact that for the last twenty years 'an impression has prevailed that a Catholic, as such, is bound to be pro-Fascist, and during the Spanish Civil War the Catholic press in nearly all countries did its best to give colour to this'. Indeed, he goes on, it 'almost escaped notice that the Basque country was solidly anti-Franco and at the same time one of the most Catholic parts of Spain' (*CWGO* 17: 220). One last point: Orwell was also certainly aware that the one country that contributed a contingent of genuine volunteers to the Francoist side in the Spanish War was Ireland in the shape of Eoin O'Duffy's 700-strong expeditionary force. Their crusade was enthusiastically cheered on by the Catholic Church. O'Duffy, 'a watery-eyed alcoholic' according to one historian (Othen 2013: 4), was the leader of the fascist Blueshirt movement in Ireland.[4] Orwell reviewed his account of the war in the *New English Weekly* on 24 November 1938, dismissing it as 'badly written and uninteresting' (*CWGO* 11: 235).

Orwell's objection to the Catholic Church remained primarily political. In his contribution to the *Partisan Review* series on 'The

PAPER

Future of Socialism', 'Towards European Unity', published in the July-August 1947 issue, he specifically identified the Catholic Church as one of the four main obstacles to the establishment of socialism in Europe. The other three were 'Russian hostility', 'American hostility' and 'Imperialism'. As far as he was concerned, if the Catholic Church survived 'as a powerful organization, it will make the establishment of true socialism impossible because its influence is and always must be against freedom of thought and speech, against human equality, and against any form of society tending to promote earthly happiness' (CWGO 19: 166). This was a hostility that he shared with Sean O'Casey!

IRISH WRITERS

While Orwell's knowledge of Irish history was slight, he was both fascinated and influenced by a number of Irish writers. Jonathan Swift's *Gulliver's Travels* (1726) was, he acknowledged on one occasion, the book that 'has meant more to me than any other book ever written'. Indeed, he wrote extensively about Swift and (in a wonderful leap of the imagination) even interviewed the man on the BBC on 2 November 1942, nearly 200 years after his death (CWGO 14: 156-161)! As well as Swift, he wrote quite extensively about Oscar Wilde, James Joyce, W. B. Yeats and Bernard Shaw.

JONATHAN SWIFT: 'ONE OF THE WRITERS I ADMIRE WITH LEAST RESERVE'

First Swift: Orwell's substantial essay, 'Politics and Literature' in the journal, *Polemic*, in September-October 1946, focused on *Gulliver's Travels*. Here, Orwell characterised Swift as 'one of those people who are driven into a sort of perverse Toryism by the follies of the progressive party of the moment', something that he could at least partly sympathise with. More generally, he saw him as someone who came to exult in his pessimism regarding humanity and, as a result, ended up as a 'reactionary' actually wanting 'to prevent Society from developing in some direction in which his pessimism may be cheated'. In the end, his pessimism sent him mad. Orwell makes clear that as far as politics and morality were concerned, 'I am against Swift', but at the same time he was 'one of the writers I admire with least reserve' and he had read *Gulliver's Travels* at least 'half a dozen times'.

But Orwell does not, however, consider Swift in an Irish context and, indeed, nowhere does he discuss Swift's *A Modest Proposal*, published in 1729, and the circumstances that could possibly produce such a savage satire. The pamphlet was reprinted in the first volume of Reginald Reynolds' edited collection *British Pamphleteers* to which Orwell contributed an 'Introduction', but he only mentions it in passing. As Reynolds points out, Swift, who usually showed such scorn for the Catholic Irish, in *A Modest Proposal* 'expressed as bitter satire the compassion he felt for their sufferings' (Orwell and Reynolds 1948: 226). What of Swift's influence on Orwell? Arthur Koestler interestingly described Orwell as 'a sort of missing link between Swift and Kafka', a remark that certainly captures something, at least, of the spirit of *Nineteen Eighty-Four* (Coppard and Crick 1984: 169).

OSCAR WILDE: ORWELL'S 'NATURAL SYMPATHY FOR THE DEFEATED'

What of Oscar Wilde? According to George Woodcock, Orwell was 'very pro-Wilde' and particularly admired '*Dorian Gray*, absurd though it is'. He put this down as being 'based mostly on his natural sympathy for the defeated' (ibid: 206). Once again though, Orwell never placed Wilde in an Irish context and was, moreover, unsure of what his contribution to literature really amounted to. Did it go beyond 'those rather cheap witticisms which used to be called epigrams' which are 'stuck all over his writings as arbitrarily as the decorations on a cake'? Wilde made his name by laughing at, by debunking, 'Victorian conventions', but, in the end, Victorian society had its revenge 'when Wilde was sent to prison for a sexual offence' (*CWGO* 15: 337). The experience destroyed him. Orwell's scepticism regarding his literary contribution did not, however, extend to his *The Soul of Man under Socialism* (1891), which Orwell reviewed in the *Observer* on 9 May 1948. Here, he characterised Wilde's vision of socialism as 'Utopian and anarchistic', imagining a world where suffering and exploitation had been abolished, where everyone had a comfortable life, where freedom prevailed and where everyone was able to realise their full capabilities, where everyone was an artist 'each striving after perfection in the way that seemed best to him'.

This, as Orwell points out, is a long way from what passed for socialism in 1948. Wilde's mistake was to believe that 'the world is immensely rich and is suffering chiefly from maldistribution'. Redistribute wealth equally and there will be plenty for everyone. This belief was widely held on the Left in the late nineteenth century, but, Orwell argues, it left 'the fearful poverty of Africa and Asia' out of the equation. Factor this poverty in and equality meant not a world of plenty but of 'common misery'. For Wilde's vision to be capable of realisation the world would have to be 'not only far richer but also technically far more advanced than the present one'. Socialism necessitated a great increase in productivity as well as equality. Nevertheless, he felt that Wilde's vision was still valuable because of the danger of dictatorship, of Socialism coming to mean 'concentration camps and secret police forces'. This is 'what has happened in Soviet Russia'. Wilde's pamphlet and others like it had the virtue that they 'demand the impossible…and remind the Socialist movement of its original, half-forgotten objective of human brotherhood' (*CWGO* 19: 333-334).

JOHN NEWSINGER

JAMES JOYCE: HOW *ULYSSES* GAVE ORWELL AN 'INFERIORITY COMPLEX'

Orwell's attitude towards James Joyce changed over time, as his own interests and concerns changed. When he was writing *A Clergyman's Daughter*, (1935), he admitted that he was obsessed with Joyce and with *Ulysses* (1922) in a letter to Brenda Salkeld. While *Ulysses* 'isn't everybody's money … personally I think it is superb in places'. He went on to confess that 'Joyce interests me so much that I can't stop talking about him once I start'. He wrote to her again some months later complaining that *Ulysses* was giving him 'an inferiority complex', that it made him 'feel like a eunuch' and that he wished he 'had never read it' (*CWGO* 10: 328, 348). And, indeed, his attempt to emulate Joyce in the celebrated/notorious Trafalgar Square episode of *A Clergyman's Daughter* was something of a disaster. When Victor Gollancz was preparing the book for publication, he sent a proof copy to Sean O'Casey, requesting a favourable quote for the dust jacket. O'Casey later remembered that the book was recommended to him by the publisher on the ground that 'they were sure the scene in Trafalgar Square was one of the most imaginative pieces of writing they had ever read – equal to Joyce at his best'. He refused, 'saying I couldn't agree with the publisher's pinnacled praise of it … the scene in Trafalgar Square wasn't even imitation Joyce'. Indeed, 'Orwell had as much chance of reaching the stature of Joyce as a tit has of reaching that of an eagle' (O'Casey 1973: 105-106). While this account is certainly coloured by O'Casey's later detestation of Orwell, he did seriously believe that it was this refusal that provoked Orwell's hostile review of his third volume of autobiography, *Drums under the Window* (1945) some ten years later. O'Casey himself was certainly capable of nursing a grudge for that long, although his later attack on Orwell was also informed by his Stalinist politics. But that settling of personal grudges was not usually Orwell's way and he had himself come to regret ever publishing *A Clergyman's Daughter*. As we shall see, he had, in fact, plenty of other more political grounds for his hostile and, it has to be said, completely unfair review.[5]

Orwell returned to Joyce in a review he wrote of Harry Levin's study, *James Joyce* (1941), that appeared in the *Manchester Evening News* on 2 March 1944. Here, he wrote of the division among even Joyce's 'declared followers' regarding *Finnegan's Wake* (1939). Was it a 'masterpiece or … simply an elephantine crossword puzzle, product of emotional sterility'. He dismisses *Dubliners* (1914) as 'slight … often clumsy', although the last story in the book, 'The Dead', is acknowledged as 'one of the most touching stories in English'. By now even *Ulysses* has been relegated to the merely 'relatively intelligible' and Orwell judges it 'difficult'; indeed, 'it is impossible to be completely certain what it is aiming at'. He goes on: 'Some of the incidents are tiresome and unconvincing, and again and again the story is overwhelmed or diverted by mere literary cleverness.' One cannot help feeling that this was a temptation that Orwell had deliberately chosen to resist after *A Clergyman's Daughter* and this decision now informed his reading of Joyce. He was, needless to say, unimpressed by *Finnegan's Wake* (*CWGO* 16: 109-111). Interestingly, he returned to Joyce a few days later in his 'As I Please' column in *Tribune*, writing in a much more sympathetic spirit, even hoping that before his death he might have 'brought himself to utter some non-neutral comment on Hitler – and coming from Joyce it might be quite a stinger' (*CWGO* 16: 119).

W. B. YEATS: THE PROBLEM OF HIS FASCISM

According to Paul Potts, the only two modern poets whom Orwell 'really liked were Yeats and Eliot' (Coppard and Crick 1984: 248). The problem with Yeats, though, as Orwell explained in yet another book review, this time appearing in *Horizon* in January 1943, was that his tendency was 'Fascist' and that this had been true 'long before Fascism was ever even heard of'. Yeats had 'the outlook of those who reach Fascism by the aristocratic route. He is a great hater of democracy ... above all, of the idea of human equality'. He quotes Yeats as longing for 'an aristocratic civilisation in its most completed form, every detail of life hierarchical, every great man's door crowded at dawn by petitioners, great wealth everywhere in a few men's hands, all dependent upon a few, up to the Emperor himself, who is a God dependent on a greater God, and everywhere, in Court, in the family, an inequality made law'.

Orwell makes the point that whereas fascist politicians would deny that this was their vision, Yeats, the poet, feels free to celebrate it quite openly. His review provoked considerable controversy, not just in *Horizon* but in the *Times Literary Supplement* as well. Orwell responded to criticism of his bringing political concerns into discussions of poetry, insisting that poetry did not exist 'in a sort of water-tight or rather thought-tight world of its own'. He insisted, quite correctly, that political and religious beliefs 'always ... colour aesthetic achievements' and that tracing 'the connexion is one necessary function of criticism'. As far as denials of Yeats's fascist sympathies were concerned, 'the facts are notorious. Did not Yeats write a "marching song" for O'Duffy's Blueshirts?' (*CWGO* 14: 279-286).[6]

BERNARD SHAW: GUILTY OF A 'SHALLOW FABIAN PROGRESSIVISM'

Bernard Shaw was, of course, a very different proposition from W. B. Yeats as far as both literature and politics were concerned. Nevertheless, Orwell never really had much to say in favour of the Fabian playwright. In the spring of 1933, he wrote to Brenda Salkeld, describing Shaw as 'Carlyle and water ... he ought to have been a Quaker (cocoa and commercial dishonesty)'. Shaw had 'squandered what he may have had back in the '80s in inventing metaphysical reasons for behaving like a scoundrel'. His only function now 'is to console fat women who yearn to be highbrows' (*CWGO* 10: 307). He was still hostile to Shaw when he broadcast a talk, 'The Rediscovery of Europe' on the BBC on 10 March 1942 (a shortened version of the talk was published in *The Listener*). Here, he accused Shaw, among others, of 'complete unawareness of anything outside the contemporary English scene'. On top of that, Shaw had no sense of history, was guilty of a 'shallow Fabian progressivism' and hoped to turn the world into 'a sort of super garden city'. He and his generation of writers were trapped in a 'backwater', but from the 1920s on English writing had once more got 'back into history'. This talk provoked considerable controversy, including two devastating responses from Robert Nichols. As he insisted, Shaw, among others, was 'detested and feared by "Society" and the propertied class as no contemporary of Mr Orwell is by any class' (*CWGO* 13: 212, 214, 216, 220).

One cannot help thinking that when he came to broadcast a talk on Shaw's *Arms and the Man* (1894) once again on the BBC, the following year, this controversy had led Orwell to modify his views. Now he was more complimentary, describing the play as 'the wittiest play he ever wrote, the most faultless technically, and, in spite of being a light comedy, the most telling'. The problem with Shaw, though, was that he was 'a debunking writer' and that as time passed his attack has 'lost something of its sting'. He points to *John Bull's Other Island* (1904) as an instance of what he means: 'The satire in this play depends largely on Ireland being under English rule, a state of affairs that has long ceased to exist.' Even so, every one of Shaw's early plays is 'equally brilliant in execution … a masterpiece of technique, with never a false note or wasted word'. And he goes on to praise Shaw for having helped to eliminate many of the hypocrisies, prejudices and abuses that he had dramatised. He concludes in a much more generous spirit that at least six of his plays, 'brilliantly witty comedies', will survive on their 'own merits', along with his criticism, at least one early novel and unspecified other works (*CWGO* 14: 323-326).

O'CASEY AND ORWELL

Sean O'Casey (1880-1964) was one of the most remarkable writers of his times, a former labourer who became an internationally playwright. He was a Dublin Protestant, born into a lower middle class family who were plunged into poverty when his father died. O'Casey grew up resigned to a hard life as a casual labourer, but threw himself into political and trade union activity. He was a member of the underground revolutionary organisation, the Irish Republican Brotherhood (IRB), and became an activist in the Irish Transport and General Workers Union (ITGWU). The Dublin Lockout of 1913 led to him breaking with the IRB over that organisation's refusal to support the locked out workers and he became, instead, a convinced 'Larkinite', a strong supporter of the ITGWU and of its leader, Big Jim Larkin. For O'Casey, the ITGWU was the instrument for the liberation of the Irish working class from class oppression and of the Irish people from national oppression. He was very actively involved during the months of the lockout, serving as secretary of the union's relief committee, a massive task, keeping thousands of locked out workers fed, clothed and housed, and as secretary of the union's militia, the Citizen Army. The Citizen Army had been established to protect pickets and demonstrations from attacks by the police and by armed scabs, attacks in which a number of workers were killed and hundreds were injured. He also wrote regularly for the union newspaper, the *Irish Worker*. This struggle was the decisive event in shaping O'Casey's world-view.

Once the ITGWU had been defeated and Larkin had left for the United States where he was to help found the Communist Party of the USA, O'Casey fell out with Jim Connolly, the union's new general secretary, resigning as secretary of the Citizen Army in protest against its alliance with the IRB. When the Citizen Army joined the IRB in staging the Easter Rising in 1916, O'Casey stood aside, condemning Connolly for abandoning the socialist cause and sacrificing working class interests in the struggle for a bourgeois republic. As far as he was concerned, the situation of working people would not be improved by gaining independence unless the working class itself came to power and it was this that the workers should be fighting for. The real hero of 1916, as far as O'Casey was concerned, was the pacifist feminist Francis Sheehy-Skeffington (1878-1916), summarily executed by the British during the fighting. It was the revolutions in Russia in 1917 that were to show the way forward for the working class.[7]

With Larkinism defeated and the ITGWU in the hands of men who, as far as O'Casey was concerned, were quite happy with the status quo and had no intention of changing the world, he turned to drama. Without any doubt, the support and encouragement he received from Lady Gregory and others were vital in his success. But in 1923, when he was in his early forties, O'Casey had his play *The Shadow of a Gunman* put on at the Abbey Theatre, Dublin, to be followed by *Juno and the Paycock* in 1925 and, most controversially, by *The Plough and the Stars*, a powerful dramatisation of his 'Larkinite' critique of the Easter Rising, in 1926. The play opened in London while the General Strike and Miners' Lockout were being fought out and O'Casey had a day's receipts donated to the Miners' Union, although the management drew the line at allowing speeches from the stage (Murray 2004: 190). Despite his success, O'Casey found independent Ireland an increasingly uncongenial environment, politically, culturally and, not least, because of the growing influence of the Catholic Church. He was to have his first book, *Windfalls*, banned in Catholic Ireland at the end of 1934.

JOHN NEWSINGER

It was not the last. He moved to Britain to live and, although he had long been sympathetic to the Soviet Union, it was only as the 1930s progressed that he embraced the Communist Party and the politics of the Popular Front. The outbreak of the Spanish Civil War in 1936 seems to have been decisive in getting him to become politically active once again. He told his publisher, Harold Macmillan (later Conservative Prime Minister) of all people, that he wished he could go and fight himself, but he had no knowledge of firearms, although he had thrown 'stones at the police' in 1913 (Krause 1975: 642). He became a regular contributor to the Communist Party's newspaper, the *Daily Worker*, serving on its editorial board from 1940 until 1952. He became a strong advocate of Stalin's Russia, contributing under the pseudonym 'Green Searchlight' to Soviet publications.

On 9 March 1938, Malcolm Muggeridge, a disillusioned socialist, who had been the *Manchester Guardian*'s Moscow correspondent in 1932-1933, published an article, 'Significance of the Soviet Trials' in the *Daily Telegraph*, condemning the Moscow Trials as a travesty and a frame-up. O'Casey wrote a reply, 'The Sword of the Soviet', supporting the trials which the *Telegraph* refused to print whereupon it appeared in the *Daily Worker* on 25 March 1938. In its turn, the *Daily Worker* refused to print Muggeridge's letter replying to O'Casey and the controversy subsequently extended to the ILP newspaper, *Forward*, which finally carried Muggeridge's devastating reply on 30 April 1938. Here Muggeridge expressed his amazement at what he called O'Casey's 'folly', marvelling that he actually believed 'confessions often containing obvious absurdities (as at the Ramzin trial, when interviews were confessed to with men dead at the time the interviews were supposed to have taken place), unsupported by documentary or other evidence … that Yagoda, in his capacity as head of the GPU, was discovering traitors at the same time as, in his other capacity as a German-Japanese spy, he was being one' and so on. If these travesties were being perpetrated in British, German or Irish courts, O'Casey would 'be the first to laugh them to scorn'. He ended that while there were people whose support for the trials was not unexpected, from 'the author of *The Juno and the Paycock* – I admit I was surprised' (Krause 1975: 717-718). Orwell almost certainly knew of this controversy although he never participated in it. And O'Casey's Stalinism survived the Hitler-Stalin Pact of 1939; indeed, seems to have been strengthened by it. He was enthusiastically in favour, endorsing the partition of Poland in 1939, urging Britain to come to terms with Nazi Germany and when Hitler finally attacked the Soviet Union in June 1941 expressing his shock: 'I thought Hitler would go Left' (Krause 1975: 891). Much later, he was to support the Soviet invasion of Hungary in 1956.

As far as Orwell was concerned, when he reviewed O'Casey's *Drums under the Window* in October 1945, he was reviewing a book by someone who was by this time at best a Stalinist hack. Even so, it was not something that he put much effort into. The review is a shabby casual hatchet-job on a fine book.[8] He dismisses the quality of the writing, 'a sort of Basic Joyce', condemns what he describes a O'Casey's 'romantic nationalism which he manages to combine with Communism' and questions why someone who appeared to hate England so much was living in Devon. The last point he made urged that guilt at British conduct in Ireland should not 'cause us to mistake a bad or indifferent book for a good one' (*CWGO* 17: 331-332). The review would hardly be worth paying attention to were it not for the ferocity of O'Casey's response. He devoted a chapter of his last volume of autobiography, *Sunset and Evening Star*, originally published in 1954, to posthumously abusing Orwell, not just for his review, but also for his hostility to Stalinism.[9] It has to be seen as part of the systematic denigration of Orwell carried out by the Communist Party and its fellow travellers.

O'Casey's 'Rebel Orwell' chapter condemned Orwell as someone who, when he was 'dying ... wanted the living world to die with him'. It was this that had produced his 'book of beasts' and when that 'didn't satisfy his yearning ego, he prophetically destroyed the world and people in Nineteen hundred and eighty four: Doomsday Book'. Far from being some kind of rebel, Orwell was rather 'a yielding blob that buried itself away from the problems of the living that all life has to face and overcome. No fight in him; always running away and yielding'. He was 'this poor wailer among the rebels' and his writing was just 'a bastard ballet of Lamentation'. As for him going 'down and out', the dish-washing tired 'him in less than a week'. Certainly, Orwell's review still infuriated him: he described it as an 'agonized yell' and went on to complain: 'Basic Joyce! Bad or good; right or wrong, O'Casey's always himself,' but the chapter is, in fact, politically driven. It ends in an embarrassing fantasy sequence in the Rose and Crown pub where Cathleen ni Houlihan (the mythical symbol of Irish nationalism) puts in an appearance and the 'dour' Orwell finally dissolves into vapour, leaving 'nothing but a slightly darker air hovering' over where he had sat and everyone else enjoying themselves (O'Casey 1973: 99-111). Unknown to O'Casey, he, together with two other Irish writers, Peadar O'Donnell and Liam O'Flaherty, had been included in Orwell's notorious compilation of fellow travellers. O'Casey was dismissed as 'Very stupid' (*CWGO* 20: 252).[10] It is a tragedy, if only a paltry one, that these two writers were separated from each other by Stalinism.

CONCLUSION

Orwell came home from Burma in 1927 a critic and opponent of the British Empire or the 'Pox Britannica' as he was to label it in his novel *Burmese Days*. This is generally acknowledged. What is less widely acknowledged is that while he supported nationalist movements that fought for independence against British imperialism, he was, nevertheless, not a great admirer of either these nationalist movements or of their leaders. They were not socialist movements, as far as he was concerned, fighting for a democratic, classless society, but rather nationalist movements that would most likely replace British oppression and exploitation with home-grown oppression and exploitation.

Indeed, as I have argued elsewhere, a good case can be made that U Po Kyin, the monstrous Burmese magistrate, portrayed in *Burmese Days*, is one of the first literary portrayals of a neo-colonialist politician fattening himself at the expense of his own people that we have. Even with regard to those communist-led movements fighting for national independence, Orwell was never going to have mistaken them for socialism. Unlike Raymond Williams, for example, he would never have mistaken Pol Pot for a socialist (Newsinger 1999: 10, 123-124). Orwell's critical attitude towards nationalist movements and their limitations is worth keeping in mind, particularly, as this paper has argued, when considering his views on Ireland and the Irish.

NOTES

[1] The best account of the protests against O'Casey's *The Plough and the Stars* and their aftermath is in Murray (2004: 171-179). Here he makes clear the Republican inspiration behind the 'riots' and the crucial role played by Hanna Sheehy-Skeffington and other Republican women. Interestingly, the 23-year-old Ria Mooney, who played Rosie Redmond, did not know what prostitution was or what a prostitute actually did for a living!

[2] The Chorley volume was to be republished in the United States in 1973 as a contribution to the debates and controversies occasioned by the Vietnam War. Chorley, herself, was to become Baroness Chorley in 1945 when her husband was made a peer by Clement Attlee and became a Labour whip in the House of Lords

[3] His discussion of anti-semitism demonstrates the strengths of this essay and is worth quoting: 'There is little evidence about this at present, because the Nazi persecutions have made it necessary for any thinking person to side with the Jews against their oppressors. Anyone educated enough to have heard the word "anti-semitism" claims as a matter of course to be free of it and anti-Jewish remarks are carefully eliminated from all classes of literature. Actually, anti-semitism appears to be widespread, even among intellectuals, and the general conspiracy probably helps to exacerbate it. People of Left opinions are not immune to it, and their attitude is sometimes affected by the fact that Trotskyists and Anarchists tend to be Jews' (*CWGO* 17: 151-152). It is worth remembering that Orwell was at this time strongly opposed to Zionism, something that inevitably fuelled accusations of anti-semitism made against him

[4] For Ireland and the Spanish Civil War see McGarry (1999) and Newsinger (2001)

[5] For a discussion of Joyce's influence on Orwell's later novels, *Keep the Aspidistra Flying* and *Coming Up for Air,* see Kerrane (2007)

⁶ According to Elizabeth Cullingford's study of Yeats's fascism (1981: 144): 'For less than a year Yeats gave qualified support to the Blueshirts, but abandoned them before their collapse. When in October 1935 Mussolini invaded Abyssinia, Yeats's disillusionment with fascism was complete. ... After that date, Yeats never again, except for tactical anti- British reasons, spoke with approval of any fascist regime. Fascism also disappeared from his prophetic thinking'

⁷ For Larkinism, the Dublin Lockout and the Easter Rising, see Newsinger (2003) and for O'Casey and Larkinism, see Newsinger (1985) and Newsinger (2004)

⁸ The first three volumes of O'Casey's autobiographies, *I Knock at the Door*, *Pictures in the Hallway* and *Drums under the Window* are major works, the fourth volume, *Inisfallen Fare Thee Well*, is not so good, but the last two, *Rose and Crown* and *Sunset and Evening Star* are very poor. As one biographer puts it, the last two volumes were the 'nadir of literary infighting' (O'Connor 1988: 357). For a critical evaluation of the autobiographies see Robert Lowery (1981)

⁹ Most shamefully, O'Casey viciously satirised a desperate appeal made to him during the Soviet purges by Freda Utley, a staunch communist at the time, whose Russian husband had been arrested and had disappeared (unknown to her he had already been shot). She hoped in vain to persuade influential communist sympathisers to intercede with the Soviet authorities on her behalf (O'Casey 1973: 92-96). This is in the chapter in *Sunset and Evening Star* immediately preceding his assault on Orwell. O'Casey had already lampooned her in his 1945 play *Oak Leaves and Lavender* where, as one critic has put it, he was 'willing to excuse and even joke about gulags, forced starvation and executions. ... It is difficult to derive pleasure from a play that repeatedly uses gulags and concentration camps as a source of easy punch lines' (Moran 2013: 109-110). For Utley's own account of her efforts to save her husband, see Utley (1940: 271-273)

¹⁰ This was not the shorter list that Orwell handed over to the Information Research Department. O'Casey was not included on that list for some unknown reason

REFERENCES

Brennan, Michael (2017) *George Orwell and Religion*, London: Bloomsbury

Coppard, Audrey and Crick, Bernard (eds) (1984) *Orwell Remembered*, London: Ariel Books

Cullingford, Elizabeth (1981) *Yeats, Ireland and Fascism*, Basingstoke: Macmillan

Kerrane, Kevin (2007) Orwell's Ireland, *The Irish Review*, Nos 36 and 37 pp 14-32

Krause, David (ed.) (1975) *The Letters of Sean O'Casey 1910-1941*, Washington DC: the Catholic University of America Press

Lowery, Robert (ed.) (1981) *Essays on Sean O'Casey's Autobiographies*, Basingstoke: Macmillan

McGarry, Fearghal (1999) *Irish Politics and the Spanish Civil War*, Cork: Cork University Press

Moran, James (2013) *The Theatre of Sean O'Casey*, London: Methuen

Murray, Christopher (2004) *Sean O'Casey: Writer at Work*, Dublin: Gill and Macmillan

Newsinger, John (1985) 'In the hunger-cry of the nation's poor is heard the voice of Ireland': Sean O'Casey and politics 1908-1916, *Journal of Contemporary History*, Vol. 20, No. 2 pp 221-240

Newsinger, John (1999) *Orwell's Politics*, Basingstoke: Macmillan

Newsinger, John (2001) Blackshirts, Blueshirts and the Spanish Civil War, *Historical Journal*, Vol. 44, No. 3 pp 625-644

JOHN NEWSINGER

Newsinger, John (2003) *Rebel City: Larkin, Connolly and the Dublin Labour Movement*, London: Merlin

Newsinger, John (2004) Sean O'Casey, Larkinism and Literature, *Irish Studies Review*, Vol. 12, No. 3 pp 283-292

O'Casey, Sean (1973) *Sunset and Evening Star*, London: Pan Books

O'Connor, Gary (1988) *Sean O'Casey: A Life*, London: Atheneum

Orwell, George and Reynolds, Reginald (eds) (1948) *British Pamphleteers, Vol.1*, London: Wingate

Othen, Christopher (2013) *Franco's International Brigade: Adventurers, Fascists and Christian Crusaders*, London: Hurst

Utley, Freda (1940) *The Dream we Lost*, New York: John Day

NOTE ON THE CONTRIBUTOR

John Newsinger is joint editor of *George Orwell Studies* and Professor of Modern History at Bath Spa University. His latest book is *Hope Lies in the Proles: George Orwell and the Left*, London: Pluto Press 2018

PAPER

'A Strange Desire of Wandering': The Female Body and the Problematic Structure of *A Clergyman's Daughter*

ZHANG WEILIANG

George Orwell has not been popular with feminists. His representations of women as passive, unintelligent and bodily has been widely criticised, but perhaps not fully understood. This paper examines the representation of Dorothy's body in A Clergyman's Daughter, *Orwell's second and most experimental novel. It argues that there is an intimate relationship between the representation of the female body and the much-debated structural flaws of this novel. Dorothy's body, starved, overworked and sexually repressed, revolts in its silences, distractions and wandering. This influences the structure of the text and results in the episodic arrangement of later chapters. Orwell's concern with Dorothy's body is a humanistic one which leads him to discover in the common human body, animalistic and vigorous, a foundation for revolt. This paper finds a positive meaning in Dorothy's return to ordinary parish life, by carefully considering Orwell's 'bodily pragmatism' in its relation to modern everyday living.*

Keywords: *A Clergyman's Daughter*, female body, time, feminist critique, structural flaw, 'bodily pragmatism'

A Clergyman's Daughter is Orwell's second novel which, he said, he was 'ashamed of' and did not allow to be reprinted or translated (*CWGO* 18: 411). Bearing many traces of the literary stylistic innovations of Joyce's *Ulysses* (1922), it is Orwell's most experimental novel, with an added challenge of a female protagonist.[1] Critical reception has mainly focused on its problematic textual structures and its equally problematic female characterisation. Even Orwell himself thought the novel a failure: 'It was a good idea, but I am afraid I have made a muck of it … it is very disconnected as a whole, and rather unreal' (*CWGO* 10: 351).

This paper argues that there is an intimate relationship between the structural problems of the novel and Orwell's female characterisation, focusing particularly on the representation of Dorothy's body. It will start with a brief examination of the novel's critical reception to provide a context for the investigation of Orwell's representation of Dorothy's body and its possible implication in the novels' 'flawed' structure. Indeed, Dorothy's body – starved, overworked and sexually repressed – revolts in its silences, distractions and wanderings, and this influences the structure of the text in its attempt to contain and represent the sufferings of her body. The paper goes on to show how Orwell's experiment in representing the female body transcends gender oppositions and extends to include the poetics of the common human body – what I call visceral language. It will end with a discussion of Orwell's 'bodily pragmatism', centred on the care for the human body and its daily living, thus giving Dorothy's final return to mediocre parish work a positive interpretation.

CRITICAL RECEPTION

In *A Clergyman's Daughter*, the heroine, Dorothy, suddenly loses her memory, finds herself on the road and finally returns home after various adventures. The novel has often been criticised for its poor structure and female characterisation. Geoffrey Stone, Orwell's contemporary reviewer, believed that the novel was composed 'under similar conditions' as Dorothy's method of pasting strip after strip of paper towards the end of the novel, resulting in a structural disconnectedness (1937 [1975: 64]). Orwell's biographer, Bernard Crick, though admitting each episode of Dorothy's adventures is 'rich, vivid and compelling', dismisses Orwell's structural experiment as 'absurdly arbitrary and implausible' (Crick 1980: 259). Giving the experiment a feminist reading, Daphne Patai observes that:

> Dorothy does not suffer from a breakdown, but a creator, Orwell, who having invented a female protagonist, does not know how to get her out of the house and into the street where he wants to place her (1984: 97).

In view of the problematic arrangement of Dorothy's sudden amnesia and departure from home, Patai suspects a much deeper and biased masculine ideology at work.[2] The structure of the novel is impaired, she believes, by Orwell's inability to understand female consciousness. Informed by Patai's feminist criticism, Robert Colls also regards the novel as 'a cross-dressing disaster' (2013: 39).

Orwell's own comment on *A Clergyman's Daughter* has probably lent weight to these critics' attacks. The source of Dorothy's adventures is modelled on his own experiences. In his letter to Leonard Moore on 2 May 1936, Orwell reported that:

> … the passages relating to hop-picking and to nights spent in Trafalgar Square were drawn directly from my own experience, & the part about the third-rate girls' school was imaginatively

reconstructed from my own experiences in third-rate boys' schools (*CWGO* 10: 479).

Robert Lee specifies the structural problem of the novel as 'its so-called documentary interpolations and its episodic structure' (1963: 23). In order to make room for Orwell's journalistic and documentary passages, Dorothy has to be drained of her memories, consciousness and even sexuality. This results in obscuring her as a character and disrupting the novel's narrative structure.

Despite all these criticisms, Patrick Reilly legitimises Dorothy's breakdown as the result of 'unremitting torture of making ends meet, the long hours of tedious labour' while he suggests the novel's structure is complete and conclusive in viewing Dorothy's journey as 'a record of faith ceding to understanding, belief to knowledge' (1986: 120). Impressed by Reilly's analysis, Peter Davison also considers Dorothy's 'odyssey' as 'concluding' (1996: 64). And Loraine Saunders defends Dorothy's amnesia as plausible by detailing early signs of her breakdown. Echoing Reilly and Davison, she contends that the novel is, in fact, 'tightly constructed … especially when considered in relation to the idea of Dorothy's "odyssey"' (2008: 63). The suggestion of a female odyssey in all the three critics, highlighting an active involvement of a female agent in the novel's structure, is an important inspiration to this paper when it attempts to investigate the relationship between the representation of the female body and the novel's structural problems.

DOROTHY'S CLOSED FEMININITY

Dorothy is neither an active character nor a sophisticated speaker. She expects things to happen to her rather than initiating them herself, and she often appears to be struggling with words, slow in her replies. Orwell's characterisation does seem to follow conventions of gender representation. This would seem to confirm feminist suspicions that patriarchy views women as bodies (rather than minds), and as static (rather than active). But it does not necessarily follow, from the fact that he uses these conventions, that Orwell is simply reproducing oppressive masculine ideology, as Patai argues. Instead, it is worth asking just what kind of femininity emerges from this emphasis on the body, and whether Dorothy is portrayed as a docile servant within a man's world, or someone much more interesting.

Orwell establishes an intimate relationship between Dorothy's femininity and her body in the scene of her waking up from the sleepwalk. Upon regaining her consciousness while inspecting her surroundings and her own existence, 'her fingertips brushed against her body', as if calling her body into material existence by the very act of touching. And this inspires her continued exploration until 'her hands encountered breasts' (*CWGO* 3: 87). At this encounter, Dorothy immediately recognises herself as a woman. The breasts reassure her female identity. The breasts, as Iris Young calls them 'a primary badge of sexual specificity, the irreducibility of sexual difference to a common measure', are prioritised as the primary determinant in Dorothy's gender identification. Young explains the symbolic significance of female breasts as 'the value of nurturing' and 'an ethic of caring' (1998 [2014: 111, 117]). Orwell's notion of femininity is implicated in an ethics of caring for the sufferings of the body. Large women figure frequently in his novels (Mrs Turle in *A Clergyman's Daughter*, and the female prisoner and the singing prole woman in *Nineteen Eighty-Four*), and possess genuine motherly attributes such as commiseration, generosity and protection. These attributes are centred on an ethics of caring which is often found lacking in Orwell's insecure, cynical and almost childish male characters. Notably, these large, motherly women are outcasts and outlaws, mostly found, not in families, but among tramps, prostitutes and criminals. The association of femininity with reproduction is often downplayed in his novels. In the society of *Nineteen Eighty-Four*, rigorous regulations and censorship reduce sex to the mere purpose of reproduction. The female body is mechanically disposed and exploited to reinforce the Party's rule. The pleasure principle of the female body in revolt endorsed by Julia (who becomes Winston Smith's lover), however, is not embraced by Dorothy whose rigid Anglican upbringing has both reduced and confined her bodily experiences to ascetic practices and actual self-harm.

Dorothy experiences her own body as closed. This is mostly reflected in her fear of sexual pleasure. It is said (in testimony to the young Orwell's interest in Freud) to have been caused by the childhood trauma of having witnessed parental intercourse. Orwell refers to Dorothy's fear as 'the especial, incurable disability', an abnormality that she fails to recognise but has to live with (*CWGO* 3: 80). The root of her fear lies in the physical violence involved in the pursuit of sexual pleasure: 'To be kissed or fondled by a man – to feel heavy male arms about her and thick male lips bearing upon her own – was terrifying and repulsive to her' (ibid). The male violence in intimate bodily pursuits breeds in her an aversion to sex and a compulsion to protect and even discipline her body.

Ascetic practices such as cold baths on freezing mornings or pricking herself with pins are performed to keep her body in control and dispel indecent thoughts. She fashions her own body as a closed space, free of male contamination. But, unfortunately, her effort elicits a completely different effect. It makes her 'the kind of girl that men habitually pester' (ibid: 81). Mr Warburton, the town rascal and long-time wooer of Dorothy, treats her body as something to constrain, even 'consume' with his touching:

> There was something very revealing, very characteristic in the way he did it; it was the lingering, appraising touch of a man to whom a woman's body is valuable precisely in the same way as though it were something to eat (ibid: 77).

Dorothy's body is cast in constant crisis because of the sexual harassment performed in various forms of touching (rubbing, mauling, pinching, kissing). Orwell presents Dorothy's bodily power of revolt in those moments of her rejection of Mr Warburton, when she flinches or disentangles herself from his overbearing sexual advances. When Dorothy is about to leave Mr Warburton's apartment after her night visit, out of the blue, she is forcibly kissed by him. In reaction to this unexpected kiss, she 'took out her handkerchief and scrubbed the place … vigorously enough to bring the blood into her cheek … until she had quite rubbed out the imaginary stain which his lips had left there' (ibid: 80).

Besides these direct encounters with men, Orwell reveals the threats to Dorothy's femininity from an ideological perspective, namely, her religious faith. Religious rituals such as communion require devotion to a physically absent God, and teach the faithful to aspire to a condition in which the body, sinful and vile, can be transcended by pure spirit. Dorothy's faith is constantly tested by the visceral reaction of her own body. She is either distracted or disgusted by the filthy physical details of the church and the unpleasant smells of the parish households. Her sensitive observation of the unsanitary procedure in taking the chalice after old Miss Mayfill prevents her from stepping to the altar. In her religious debate with Mr Warburton, his illustrations of the neglect to the sufferings of the physical body in Christianity render her speechless. Christianity, Orwell seems to suggest, aims at a spiritual transcendence beyond the physical body. It disciplines her body into obedience and oblivion. But eventually her body reacts back.

'STRANGE DESIRE OF WANDERING': SPATIAL AND BODILY REVOLT

The sound of an alarm clock going off starts *A Clergyman's Daughter*, waking up Dorothy in extreme physical exhaustion. For the service of her father and the Father in Heaven, her parish work puts pressure on Dorothy in the form of the tyranny of time, a patriarchal time that governs her days. The novel's first chapter sketches out a woman's life in one day when time reigns over and represses her fatigued body, gradually breaking down to a hypnotic point of sleepwalking. The alarm clock in her bedroom, with its 'nagging feminine clamour', symbolises her already interiorised sense of patriarchal time that automatically nudges her to keep on track, while towards the end of this chapter, 'the grandfather clock in her father's study struck midnight', ending the day for her with no chance of escape but mountains of tasks yet to carry out (CWGO 3: 1, 84). At the end of the novel, Orwell carefully indicates that a charwoman's broom-handle has been put through 'the face of the grandfather clock in the study' (ibid: 254). The return of the faithless heroine is accompanied by a violent rejection of patriarchal time.

But, significantly, it is in this first chapter when Dorothy rebels against the daily routine. In order to be punctual for tidying up her father's study, she throws on her attire 'in the space of about three minutes' (CWGO 3: 5). To facilitate her morning visits around the parish, her old bicycle lends her freedom by swiftly traversing different spaces[3] so that her wandering disrupts the tyranny of time and its scheduled linear arrangement of her tasks.

Orwell instances two occasions of Dorothy's wandering, one to the dairy-farmer's meadow and the other to Mr Warburton's house at night. Dorothy is lured away to the meadow by the 'scent of cows, like a distillation of vanilla and fresh hay', a scent which contrasts with the vile smells in the parish households (ibid: 55). Her sensory immersion in the richness of the natural landscape throws her into a mystical joy of ecstasy. It delivers her from from bodily fatigue and displaces her to a Romantic, faraway landscape. The scent of fennel in the 'summery fume' reminds her of childhood joys and transports her to 'spice-drenched islands in the warm foam of oriental seas', a remote and mysterious space that owes something to Keatsian fantasy – 'Charm'd magic casements, opening on the foam / of perilous seas, in faery lands forlorn' (ibid: 55; Keats 1819 [1994: 220]).

The other wandering takes her to Mr Warburton's house at night. It is quite scandalous for a clergyman's daughter to visit a womaniser's apartment at night, though Dorothy is cheated into visiting, thinking there would be others there to keep her company. But then the imperative to leave Mr Warburton's house remains in her conscious thought yet is never put into immediate action. The reason is a bodily one: 'chiefly because she was horribly tired and the leather armchair into which Mr Warburton had thrust her the moment she entered the house was too comfortable to leave' (op cit: 74). Bodily comfort is prioritised, despite the jabs of her conscience, over the scandalous implication entailed in her overstaying. Her fatigue, a message from the body, has held her back, and has proved stronger than the injunctions of both religion and society about how an unmarried woman should behave.

AMNESIA AND APHASIA

Dorothy's fatigue and her strange desire of wandering finally lead her astray, away from the entangled perplexities of meaning, faith and redemption, into a state of amnesia. She is tranced into unconscious, and her body, unbridled and free, hypnotically wanders away from Suffolk to Kent. Orwell deliberately leaves this crucial moment of Dorothy's sleepwalk unsaid, creating a huge gap in the narrative. When fatigue strains the body to breaking point and leads it astray, language becomes, as Dorothy has felt about her prayers, 'useless, meaningless – nothing but the dead shells of words' which is better dispensed with and left out (*CWGO* 3: 10). As Dorothy's consciousness surrenders to the hallucinatory state of her body, the authoritative voice that has dominated the first chapter slides into aphasia. Her body has rendered the authoritative voice speechless, disrupts the linear narration dictated by time, and tears the arrangement of following chapters into fragmentary episodes.

The authoritative voice gradually recedes to a point of total disappearance in the dramatic Trafalgar Square scene. These fragmentary episodes, retelling her vagrancy, hop-picking and teaching, are neatly threaded by Dorothy's bodily experiences of fatigue, hunger and cold. In these episodes, Orwell manages, on the one hand, to probe into social predicaments and moral obstacles to female employment in a male world, and on the other hand, to experiment with a form of poetic language that particularly belongs to the body.

THE COMMON BODY

Dorothy's adventures have borne witness to the social predicaments of women's independence, exemplified mostly by her female employers who have chosen middle-class decency over pity and sympathy towards her hunger-stricken body in its down-and-out raggedness. Orwell's major concern over Dorothy's adventures is a humanistic one and a bodily one. Being so focused on the human body, it is not surprising that his characterisation of Dorothy is attentive to her physical nature and condition. Dorothy's body, starved and pained, not only bears the signs of affliction, but also a capacity for resistance to the forces – patriarchal, capitalist and tyrannical – which always threaten to exhaust and deform it.

Suggestions of fatigue, hunger and sleeplessness persist throughout the novel. In contrast to the misery and pressure inflicted by her parish work at home, Dorothy's long and laborious work in the hop field, immersed 'in strong sunlight, in the sound of forty voices singing, in the smell of hops', restores inside her 'a physical joy, a warm satisfied feeling' (*CWGO* 3: 114). This is still alienated labour, yet for her body it is a kind of liberation, indeed a version of Keats' utopia of 'a life of sensations rather than of thoughts' (1817 [1935: 68]). The sunburnt feeling mingled with sound and smell provokes a surge of emotions:

> It was a life that wore you out, used up every ounce of your energy, and kept you profoundly happy … the coarse food and insufficient sleep, the smell of hops and wood smoke, lulled you into an almost beastlike heaviness. Your wits seemed to thicken,

just as your skin did, in the rain and sunshine and perpetual fresh air (op cit: 121).

The communal work, though repetitive and exhaustive, enlivens the body into sensory interaction with the outward environment. The interaction is simultaneously an immersion and liberation. It trances the body into its vigorous animality, 'the beastlike heaviness'. These sensory feelings, 'dazed and witless', caused mostly by sleep deprivation and prolonged exposure in the open air, revisit Dorothy in the Trafalgar Square episode: 'The world, inner and outer, grows dimmer till it reaches almost the vagueness of a dream' (ibid: 186).

A VISCERAL LANGUAGE

The Trafalgar Square episode is the most celebrated part of the novel for its structural innovations with monologues and dialogues intersecting and intermingling each other. Dorothy loses her position as protagonist when her voice is reduced to an occasional complaint about the numbness of her feet and her body submerges among those of the tramps.[4] The booming dramatic voices from the tramps, performed in various speech acts (complaining, begging, swearing, teasing, preaching and singing), are of a visceral nature. Bodily metaphors and allusions seep into their utterances, demonstrating an embodied understanding of the vast material world where their miserable fate is physically felt and shared. The motherly Mrs McElligot complains that the bench she lies on 'catch[es] you across de kidneys'; the deserted Mrs Bendigo curses her husband and still cannot 'stomach' the maltreatment of her eviction from home and marriage; the unemployed Snouter swears at his wage-withholding employers and threatens to 'cut it [kip] out of their bowels' (ibid: 155-157).

Orwell's emphasis on the tramps' pet phrase 'bloody' is thus to be read as not only an expression of swearing, but also a corporeal register of the vigour and vitality of their demotic speech. In 'Propaganda and Demotic Speech' (1944), Orwell equates demotic speech with 'simple, concrete language', 'everyday language', 'spoken English' and 'ordinary slipshod, colloquial English'. This contrasts sharply with the 'bloodless dialect of government spokesmen' and the 'deadly' and 'educated' upper-class accent (CWGO 16: 310-316). The bodily metaphors that have crept into the tramps' habitual utterances infuse their speech with energy and freshness. The pronounced physical heaviness makes their cockney-accented speech genuinely accessible and poetically rich.

As night falls, these voices are obscured and disintegrated into 'a chorus of varying sounds – groans, curses, bursts of laughter and singing, and through them all the uncontrollable chattering of teeth' (ibid: 169). To fight against the penetrating cold, the tramps resort to various bodily performances such as stamping, clapping, making a human pyramid of 'animal heat' and wrapping 'monstrous' paper cocoons (ibid: 175, 178). Orwell politicises their bodily performances by having the policeman patrol and supervise the square. The policeman's major responsibility is to prevent cold-weather casualties of the tramps to keep the square decent as a space for the public. Orwell's invention of a visceral language is founded on the particular experiences of the tramps. His artistic experiment here is checked, if not constrained, by his growing realist preoccupation with the tramps.

THE RETURN

As Orwell's novels often begin with an indication of a specific time, the theme of return is common to their endings. *A Clergyman's Daughter* ends with Dorothy's return to her old parish life of 'sameness and futility' (*CWGO* 3: 281). With her religious faith lost, the parish life – crammed with trivial tasks, visits and rituals that have to be performed accordingly and repeatedly – is without meaning and descends into mediocrity and boredom. Her world seems 'a little emptier' and a 'little poorer' (ibid: 273). Here, Orwell paints a rather pathetic picture of Dorothy, a faithless and hence hypocritical clergyman's daughter, trapped and enslaved in the daily drudgery of boredom. But as Ben Highmore observes, the boredom of everyday life can also be 'an index of unfulfilled desires and unnamed anxieties … an area of social and political struggles' (2002: 11). Unfulfilled desires and unnamed anxieties are conveyed in Dorothy's meditation over her own fate which also extends to the general womb-to-tomb human life as having 'a quality of greyness, of desolation, that could never be described, but which you could feel like a physical pang at your heart' (*CWGO* 3: 292).

This sense of greyness and desolation, beyond the realm of language but registered in the body as physical pain, points to her dissatisfaction with her meaningless parish work, a dissatisfaction that reproaches the patriarchal and capitalist society in devaluing and marginalising women's domestic work in attending the messy details of everyday life. The loss of Dorothy's faith entails an urgent need to find a replacement. But it is not to be found in her meditation, because the small tasks she is handling effectively 'changed the tenor of her thoughts' (ibid: 294). Orwell shows that any attempt to sentimentalise or rationalise everyday living is futile and falls easily into the traps of 'exaggeration and self-pity' (ibid: 294). The body, enmeshed in the complex webs of everyday life, becomes for Dorothy a ground on which she can build her new faith.

The body, in its expression of organic vitality and energy, constitutes what Michael Gardiner calls 'a focal point of resistance' against repetitive and routinised modern living (2000: 16). Gardiner's reading is informed by Henri Lefebvre (1984) and Mikhail Bakhtin

(1984) who highlight the importance of the sensuous, passionate and impulsive human body against the systematised and predictable everyday life under modernity.[5] Indeed, Dorothy's care for her body not only protects her from her old habits of arid self-discipline, but also promotes her to be willingly and actively involved in parish work in order to attend to the needs of the others. In the seemingly pathetic fate of Dorothy, Orwell make her voluntary devotion something to respect and admire.

NOTES

[1] For a discussion on Joyce's influences on Orwell, see Keith Williams (1999) and Ruth Hoberman (2015)

[2] Patai's reading has inaugurated a long line of feminist readings of Orwell who is routinely portrayed as conventional, masculine, misogynistic, sexist and even homophobic. Later feminist readings, exemplified by Janet Montefiore (1985) and Ben Clarke (2007), tend to explore Orwell's gender issues through the lenses of class, tradition, industrialism and capitalism. And contrary to the general feminist readings of Orwell, recent studies by Nalin Jayasena (2007), Eva Karpinski (2008) and Praseeda Gopinath (2013) have argued for a more complex and contested notion of masculinity (or masculinities) existing in Orwell's works

[3] Like H. G. Wells's heroine Jessie Milton in *The Wheels of Chance* (1896 [1925]), Dorothy gains a measure of freedom with her bicycle. She will intentionally put her bicycle between Mr Warburton and herself to avoid his pestering. And when conversations with Mr Warburton and Ms Semprill turn to indecent topics, she hurriedly wheels away as an escape

[4] Dorothy's glimmering presence has been read by Roger Fowler as a sign of her alienation from the tramps: 'The speech of her associates in the Square is, to her, a senseless cacophony. Speech is companionable and democratic for the other tramps, a medium of preservation, but it is for her a symbol of her alienation' (1995: 118). Fowler has recognised the cockney-accented speech but ignored the implications and effects of those bodily tropes in it. The oscillation of Dorothy's absence and presence demonstrates the dynamic process of her bodily immersion with the tramps. When the policeman sees her as a cut above all the tramps and proposes to take her away, she refuses and stays put

[5] Orwell makes use of the body's resisting power more thoroughly in *Nineteen Eighty-Four*, where the physical texture of everyday life is threatened by the Party's quest to scientifically manipulate human beings as puppets

REFERENCES

Bakhtin, Mikhail (1984) *Rabelais and His World*, Iswolsky, Hélène (trans.), Cambridge MA: MIT Press

Clarke, Ben (2007) *Orwell in Context: Communities, Myths, Values*, Basingstoke: Palgrave Macmillan

Colls, Robert (2013) *George Orwell: English Rebel*, Oxford: Oxford University Press

Crick, Bernard (1980) *George Orwell: A Life*, Harmondsworth, Middlesex: Penguin

Davison, Peter (1996) *George Orwell: A Literary Life*, London: Macmillan Press

Davison, Peter (ed.) (1998) *The Complete Works of George Orwell (CWGO)*, 20 volumes, London: Secker & Warburg

Fowler, Roger (1995) *The Language of George Orwell*, London: Macmillan Press

Gardiner, Michael (2000) *Critiques of Everyday Life*, London: Routledge

Gopinath, Praseeda (2013) *Scarecrows of Chivalry: English Masculinities after Empire*, Charlottesville: Virginia University Press

Highmore, Ben (2002) *Everyday Life and Cultural Theory: An Introduction*, London: Routledge

Hoberman, Ruth (2015) The nightmare of history in George Orwell's *A Clergyman's Daughter*, Carpentier, Martha (ed.) *Joycean Legacies*, Basingstoke: Palgrave Macmillan pp 92-111

Jayasena, Nalin (2007) *Contested Masculinities: Crises in Colonial Male Identity from Joseph Conrad to Satyajit Ray*, New York: Routledge

Karpinski, Eva (2008) En-trenched manhood: War and constructions of masculinity in George Orwell's *Homage to Catalonia*, *Men and Masculinities*, Vol. 10, No. 5 pp 523-537

Keats, John (1817 [1935]) Letter 31, Forman, Maurice (ed.) *The Letters of John Keats*, New York: Oxford University Press

Keats, John (1819 [1994]) Ode to a Nightingale, Wright, Paul (ed.) *The Poems of John Keats*, Hertfordshire: Wordsworth Editions

Lefebvre, Henri (1984) *Everyday Life in the Modern World*, Rabinovitch, Sacha (trans.), New Brunswick: Transaction Publishers

Montefiore, Janet (1996) *Men and Women Writers of the 1930s: The Dangerous Flood of History*, New York: Routledge

Patai, Daphne (1984) *The Orwell Mystique: A Study in Male Ideology*, Amherst: Massachusetts University Press

Reilly, Patrick (1986) *George Orwell: The Age's Adversary*, London: Macmillan Press

Saunders, Loraine (2008) *The Unsung Artistry of George Orwell*, Aldershot: Ashgate

Stone, Geoffrey (1937 [1975]) Review of *A Clergyman's Daughter*, Meyers, Jeffrey (ed.) *George Orwell: The Critical Heritage*, London: Routledge & Kegan Paul p. 64

Wells, H. G. (1896 [1925]) *The Wheels of Chance*, New York: Charles Scribner's Sons

Williams, Keith (1999) 'The unpaid agitator': Joyce's influence on George Orwell and James Agee, *James Joyce Quarterly*, Vol. 36, No. 4 pp 729-763

Young, Iris Marion (1998 [2014]) Breasted experience: The look and the feeling, Weitz, Rose (ed.) *The Politics of Women's Bodies: Sexuality, Appearance, Behavior*, Oxford: Oxford University Press pp 107-120

NOTE ON THE CONTRIBUTOR

Zhang Weiliang has just completed his PhD on Orwell under the supervision of Professor Douglas Kerr at the University of Hong Kong. His thesis explores the human body in Orwell's novels and proposes that Orwellian ethics is bodily. Zhang received his MA in English and American Literature at Beijing Foreign Studies University, and his BA in English at Ningbo University. His research interests include 20th-century English literature and theories of the body.

PAPER

Nineteen Eighty-Four and *Brave New World*: Complementary Visions Reconsidered

ANNA VANINSKAYA

At a time when both Nineteen Eighty-Four *and* Brave New World *are more politically relevant than ever, and when specialist academic criticism of George Orwell's and Aldous Huxley's great dystopias has reached a point of saturation, it is salutary to go back to basics and talk about these books as books on their own terms. This paper does so in order to argue that their visions are ultimately complementary and that this complementarity is enhanced by the significant contrast in the novels' tones, satirical targets, handling of influences and development of common themes. Among the latter, hope, failure, solitude and insanity emerge as the primary keys to the twin visions of a future dystopia.*

Keywords: Orwell, Huxley, *Nineteen Eighty-Four*, *Brave New World*, dystopian visions

It is exactly a century since the young Aldous Huxley taught the even younger Eric Blair at Eton.[1] That slender thread of initial association strengthened as Eric grew up to become George Orwell: he had a librarian procure Huxley's *Brave New World* as soon as it was published in 1932 (Crick 1980 [1982: 117, 221]); he invoked Huxley in his journalism, essays and letters throughout the 1930s and 40s, and finally, in 1949, he requested his publisher to send Huxley a copy of *Nineteen Eighty-Four* (Smith 1969: 604).

Orwell's admiration for *Brave New World*, like Huxley's for Orwell's dystopia, came with serious reservations. Each held that the other had isolated something critical about the operation of power in yesterday's, and perhaps today's world, but had failed imaginatively in envisioning its development in the world of tomorrow. For Orwell, Huxley's 'brilliant caricature of the present (the present of 1930)' cast 'no light on the future' (*CWGO* 12: 211);[2] for Huxley, the nightmare of *Nineteen Eighty-Four* was 'destined to modulate into the nightmare' of *Brave New World* (Smith 1969: 605). Each implied that the other's dystopia succeeded better as satire than as prophecy: a satire, in Huxley's case, of jazz-age America in the 1920s and, in Orwell's, of post-World War Two austerity England crossed with Stalinist Russia. Each posited a global future as an outgrowth of the trends in his own chosen geographical locale. And whether readers in subsequent decades have recognised their own world more readily in Huxley's consumption-driven, sensation-titillating, youth and pleasure-oriented paradise, with its 'Human Element Managers', or in the dilapidated and fear-saturated existence of Orwell's Airstrip One, has always depended primarily on the accidents of geography. In some places, the future did, indeed, look like California; in others, it resembled a lot more the eastern side of the Iron Curtain. Both dystopias have proved equally indispensable to an understanding of twentieth-century history. And now that both visions have acquired renewed relevance in the twenty-first, it pays to re-examine them in their original contexts once again. For only when seen in juxtaposition with each other and on their own terms as works of literature does their striking complementarity most clearly come to the fore.

BIOGRAPHICAL BACKGROUNDS

A brief excursion into the two authors' biographies will help to throw light on their works. Huxley was the elder by a decade, born in 1894 into a prominent family: his grandfather was the famous Victorian scientist T. H. Huxley, his great-uncle the famous Victorian poet and cultural critic Matthew Arnold, and his aunt the no-longer famous but at the time very successful novelist Mrs Humphry Ward. Huxley graduated from Oxford University during the Great War and was launched almost immediately on his career as a man of letters and a satellite figure of the Bloomsbury circle. From 1923, he spent most of his time abroad, first in southern Europe and then, from 1937, in California. He published many novels, books of essays, poetry and travel writing, and in his later years turned to mysticism, in which guise he became a guru for the Beats and hippies. Huxley died in 1963, on the same day (22 November) as President Kennedy.

Orwell was born in 1903 into the family of a colonial civil servant, and his beginnings were just as privileged as Huxley's: he attended Huxley's *alma mater* Eton, the centuries-old public school home of the British elite. But his life trajectory took an unusual swerve when, instead of going on to Oxford like his contemporaries, he enlisted in 1922 as a policeman in Burma, then part of the British Empire. His career as a writer did not properly begin until after he resigned and returned to England in 1927. In order to gather material for his books, and to expiate his guilt for serving what he came to regard as an imperial tyranny – in a move of symbolic self-flagellation that would have seemed familiar to John Savage of *Brave New World* – Orwell turned himself into a down-and-out. He lived with the homeless and wrote about his experiences in *Down and Out in*

ANNA VANINSKAYA

Paris and London (1933), a mix of memoir, fiction and documentary published the year after Huxley's hedonistic dystopia. He observed the unemployed in the Depression-ravaged north of England, and then, at the end of 1936, went to fight against Franco's fascists in the Spanish Civil War. Huxley moved to Hollywood at about the same time. During the Blitz, Orwell stayed in London working for the BBC and later *Tribune*, wrote *Animal Farm* (1945), and almost literally on his deathbed – for he was dying of the tuberculosis that had been exacerbated by his unorthodox lifestyle on a remote Scottish island and his compulsive smoking – he composed *Nineteen Eighty-Four* (1949).

Even in 1950, the year of his death, Orwell remained a committed democratic socialist, although he no longer believed in the imminence of a revolution, as he had a few years earlier. As he put it in 1946 in 'Why I Write': 'Every line of serious work that I have written since 1936 has been written, directly or indirectly, *against* totalitarianism and *for* democratic socialism' (*CWGO* 18: 320). At the time of writing *Brave New World* in 1931, Huxley was, in his own characterisation, an 'amused, Pyrrhonic aesthete' as well as a supporter of eugenics and state planning (1932 [1994: xxviii]). Before its composition, Huxley had specialised in witty dissections of the mores, ideas and lifestyles of the English *haute bourgeoisie*, always with a dash of comic caricature that would so pungently season his dystopia. Orwell, on the other hand, had alternated between gritty memoir-documentaries of the lives of tramps, soldiers and unemployed miners and naturalistic novels about the failures of lower middle-class social outcasts.

THE CONTRASTING LITERARY STYLES OF THE TWO WORKS

The tone and style of the two dystopias bear out this biographical contrast. Both writers acknowledged the essentially parodic nature of their works, but *Brave New World* is a lighter book in every sense than *Nineteen Eighty-Four*, and its serious social critique constantly tips over into farce. The World Controller makes a joking reference to lethal chambers, but he is no Big Brother: in practice, the worst that can happen to an individual who rebels against the state is exile to a poor climate among interesting people. The novel is at times gratuitously and darkly funny: a moment of romantic absent-mindedness at work can result in the death of 'a promising young Alpha-Minus administrator' twenty-two years later (ibid: 170). But more often, Huxley's humour hinges on the incongruity produced by role-reversal and unexpected juxtaposition. It is incongruous and, therefore, funny when the familiar and the respectable, the solid reference points of the status quo, are slightly estranged but still remain recognisable through the mockery: when 'our Lord' is replaced by 'our Ford' and the cross by the T of Ford's model-T car. 'Here the Director made a sign of the T on his stomach and all the students reverently followed suit' (ibid: 21). Instead of God in his

Heaven, 'Ford's in his flivver', so 'All's well with the world' (ibid: 39). The Westminster Abbey becomes a cabaret, the gentlemen's Athenaeum Club becomes the Aphroditaeum (wisdom, symbolically, giving place to sex), and the Archbishop of Canterbury becomes the Arch-Community-Songster of Canterbury (calling a spade a spade). The *Daily Mail* and *Daily Mirror* – then as now by-words for tabloid propaganda – become *The Delta Mirror* still produced, six hundred years in the future, out of Fleet Street, the London home of journalism, or as it is known in *Brave New World*: 'The various Bureaux of Propaganda and the College of Emotional Engineering' (ibid: 58). All of these are time-worn satirical devices, of a kind Orwell for the most part studiously avoids.

John Savage's reactions to the brave new world he encounters are played for laughs even at the most solemn moments. The reader's sympathies may be wholly with him when he is outraged by the chocolate-éclair-wielding twins' profanation of the mystery of death – though we may be tempted to smile in spite of our sympathy. But his quixotic attempt to force the Deltas to be free by depriving them of their soma ration, and even more so the punch-up that follows, are presented in an unabashedly comic vein. By the time the narrative arrives at its portrait of the Savage whittling his bow and arrows in his so-called 'hermitage' 'between Puttenham and Elstead' (ibid: 222), swallowing boiled mustard and embracing juniper bushes to purge his soul of wickedness while being besieged by paparazzi, it has undisguisedly entered the realm of the absurd. And in a sense, it had always been there, since all these actions spring from the absurd mishmash that is the Savage's mind: Jesus and Pookong, Shakespeare and 'the Elementary Instructions for Beta Workers in the Embryo Store' (ibid: 182), 'Heaven and London and Our Lady of Acoma and the rows and rows of babies in clean bottles and Jesus flying up and Linda flying up and the great Director of World Hatcheries and Awonawilona' (ibid: 116).

Winston Smith's mind in *Nineteen Eighty-Four* is also a mishmash of half-understood fragments, and if the Savage has his 'Streptocock-Gee to Banbury-T', Winston has his '"Oranges and lemons," say the bells of St Clement's' (*CWGO* 9: 153). Both lack a genuine, vital connection to the culture these rhymes come from, but whereas the Savage's 'A, B, C, vitamin D' has a primarily comic function (op cit: 182), Winston's nursery rhyme eventually leads to horror and darkness. Both dystopias offer a theatre of the absurd – O'Brien's statements in the torture scenes are intentionally absurdist – but Orwell's is a very different kind of absurdism from Huxley's. Perhaps a better designation for it would be theatre of cruelty.

The brave new world may be cruel as well, but it is not frightening: it is a Swiftian world, where people are 'only truly happy when they're standing on their heads' (ibid: 14) and where expected associations are continually undermined at the verbal as well as the thematic level. The narrative abounds in incongruous and oxymoronic statements: 'The air was drowsy with the murmur of bees and helicopters' (ibid: 26); Eton rears its 'venerable piles of ferro-concrete and vita-glass' (ibid: 145). Expectations are most blatantly reversed in the ticklish matter of sexual propriety, and 'healthy virtuous' English girls – the reader is meant to savour the cliché here – are expected to behave as women of loose character (ibid: 57), while 'gentleman' becomes a synonym for womaniser. The novel excels at shocking the older, conventionally minded reader while eliciting a laugh from the emancipated generation of the 1920s who prided themselves on puncturing the values of Victorian prudery:

> 'Of course there's no need to give him up. Have somebody else from time to time, that's all. He has other girls, doesn't he?'
> Lenina admitted it.
> 'Of course he does. Trust Henry Foster to be the perfect gentleman – always correct. And then there's the Director to think of. You know what a stickler ...'
> Nodding, 'He patted me on the behind this afternoon,' said Lenina.
> 'There, you see!' Fanny was triumphant. 'That shows what *he* stands for. The strictest conventionality' (ibid: 37).
>
> Lenina shook her head. 'Somehow,' she mused, 'I hadn't been feeling very keen on promiscuity lately ...' 'But one's got to make the effort,' [Fanny] said sententiously, 'one's got to play the game' (ibid: 38).

Promiscuity as the duty of the virtuous female: Huxley milks the joke for all it is worth.

Such role-reversal satire is complemented by ironic topical jabs at contemporary writers and thinkers: 'Our Ford – or Our Freud, as, for some inscrutable reason, he chose to call himself whenever he spoke of psychological matters' (ibid: 34); 'Little Reuben woke up repeating word for word a long lecture by that curious old writer ("one of the very few whose works have been permitted to come down to us"), George Bernard Shaw, who was speaking, according to a well-authenticated tradition, about his own genius' (ibid: 21). Shaw, like H. G. Wells, was part of the older generation of pre-war fathers whom the rebellious bright young things of the 1920s loved to hate. Huxley's naming conventions also have a long satirical pedigree. Every monicker is a gem of incongruity, in which good old-fashioned English names like Polly are coupled with the surnames of foreign revolutionaries like Trotsky, not to mention all the namesakes of Bakunin, Lenin, Marx, Engels, Mussolini, Hoover, Wells and the Jewish financiers and industrialists Rothschild and Alfred Mond.

Even the descriptions of bloodshed are topical caricatures dripping with black humour: 'Eight hundred Simple Lifers were mowed down by machine guns at Golders Green. ... Then came the famous British Museum Massacre. Two thousand culture fans gassed with dichlorethyl sulphide' (ibid: 44-45). Laughter, not horror, is the intended reaction. The jingles of hypnopaedic wisdom are more hilarious than chilling, as is the advertising levity injected into the description of the drug that keeps the world population in mental subjection: 'Take a holiday from reality whenever you like, and come back without so much as a headache or a mythology' (ibid: 48). The tone is flippant, amused: the reader is being treated to witticisms, not warnings. It is all too easy, in John Savage's words; the stakes, for much of the book, are not high enough.

The feel of Orwell's Airstrip One is totally different. The reader is immersed from the very first line in the dreary, dilapidated environment of a naturalistic novel: the smell of cabbage soup and of human sweat, the plugged sinks, the dust in the creases of Mrs Parsons's face, the varicose veins, the old prostitutes, the sharp wind, the oily gin, the animal fear. Unlike Huxley's parodic distancing, all these are stylistic markers of immediacy, of a near future that is meant to be indistinguishable from the present, by whose side not only the synthetic, brightly coloured playground of Huxley's far-futuristic London, but even his dirty, diseased and violent Savage Reservation look romanticised and unreal. By the time Orwell came to write *Nineteen Eighty-Four* in the late forties, he had perfected his naturalistic technique, with its detailed evocation of smell and the grossness of the human body, its attention in particular to the physical, dirty, disgusting side of life. The fetid rooms of casual wards packed with human refuse, the squatting 'natives' in the prison blocks of Burma, the dung-encrusted winter fields around the trenches in Spain, London during the Blitz: these were the raw materials that went to make up the world of *Nineteen Eighty-Four*. From the perspective of this world, the 'pneumatic' flappers, the jazz musicians and the Hollywood movies Huxley had seen during his trip to America in 1926 and used to spice up his dystopia, appear as immeasurably far away as the New Mexico Huxley got at second hand from the books of his friend D. H. Lawrence.

REINVENTING COMMON ORIGINS: UTOPIAN TARGETS

As in setting, so in ideology: Orwell's and Huxley's targets came from different hemispheres. 'I wish you had seen California,' Huxley wrote in a letter of 1927, 'Materially, the nearest approach to Utopia yet seen on our planet' (Huxley 1932 [1994: vii]). According to David Bradshaw, in his Introduction to Huxley's novel,

> Huxley reiterated his doleful prophecy that 'the future of America is the future of the world' on a number of occasions in the 1920s, and it is clear that the World State, with its huge skyscrapers,

PAPER

ANNA VANINSKAYA

dollar economy, cult of youth, 'feelies' (tactile descendants of Hollywood's talkies), sex-hormone chewing-gum, ubiquitous zippers (identified by Huxley as America's national 'crest') and wailing sexophones, was first conceived as a satire on the global diffusion of the American way of life. Huxley had discovered Henry Ford's *My Life and Work* in the ship's library during his voyage to the United States, and everything he came across after he had disembarked at San Francisco seemed perfectly in tune with Fordian principles (see Huxley 1932 [1994: vii]).

In this respect, Huxley was following in the footsteps of a writer who comes first in any chronological listing of the most significant dystopian authors of the twentieth century: the Russian Yevgeny Zamyatin. His *We* – written in the early 1920s and usually read as a critique of the beginnings of Soviet totalitarianism – actually took most of its features either from the writings of H. G. Wells, or from contemporary British and American society. Taylorism, the system of scientific management pioneered by the American theorist of industrial efficiency, Frederick Taylor, was one of its main targets. *We* influenced Orwell, though Huxley claimed never to have read it. Nevertheless, *Brave New World* effects the same reification of the processes of American modernity as *We* – the cult of Henry Ford is the state religion and his assembly-line mass production, as 'applied to biology' no less (Huxley 1932 [1994: 5]), is the ruling principle of social organisation. Demand-driven economics – several years before J. M. Keynes published his *General Theory* (1936) – is another such principle.

Keynes's cropping up here is not an accident, for *Brave New World* is, among other things, a response to the Great Depression. What is particularly curious is that in the years surrounding the writing of the book, Huxley, appalled by the disaster of the Depression, repeatedly spoke out in favour of implementing the kind of propaganda-based state control described by Mustapha Mond, supported 'an ordered universe' over 'planless incoherence' and regarded a eugenicist dictatorship as a solution to the chaos he witnessed around him (Huxley 1932 [1994: ix]). None of these ideas were new. All had been adumbrated in the writings of H. G. Wells – not just the father of science fiction, but a massively influential public figure of the early twentieth century, and the inescapable reference point for several generations of utopian and dystopian writers, including both Huxley and Orwell, who followed directly in his footsteps. Huxley advocated Wells's favoured solutions to the problems of the contemporary world, while simultaneously conceiving *Brave New World* as a novel about what he called in 1931 'the horror of the Wellsian Utopia and a revolt against it' (Smith 1969: 348).

Wells, although he began publishing in the 1880s, was still as vocal as ever in the 1920s and 30s, and had already served as a butt for Huxley's satire in his pre-*Brave New World* realist novels. This oedipal relationship was typical of Orwell as well. Contemporary readers would have easily recognised all the Wellsian clichés in Huxley's dystopia: the glittering high-rise cities, the healthy, beautiful and self-satisfied inhabitants, the caste of expert rulers at the top. But that same utopian norm was also at the back of *Nineteen Eighty-Four*, as Goldstein's book ironically reminds us: 'In the early twentieth century, the vision of a future society unbelievably rich, leisured, orderly and efficient – a glittering antiseptic world of glass and steel and snow-white concrete – was part of the consciousness of nearly every literate person' (*CWGO* 9: 196). Huxley retains this picture, but shows that there is something rotten within it: the Wellsian-American dream becomes a nightmare. But Orwell jettisons it altogether: his future society is the opposite of this vision in every particular. 'Wells is too sane to understand the modern world,' Orwell wrote in an essay called 'Wells, Hitler and the World State' (*CWGO* 12: 540), and so, by implication, was Huxley. The modern world was run by 'lunatics', irrational 'warlords' and 'witchdoctors' – by O'Brien, in other words, who is, of course, insane by any normal 'early twentieth century' standards. It was not run by efficient Alpha double-plus experts who had the welfare and happiness of society at heart. If Huxley's fear (but also, perhaps, hope) in 1931 – before Hitler and Franco, before the war – was the realisation of the Wellsian-American utopia,[3] Orwell's fear in the 1940s was that it was irretrievably out of date, superseded by a state of affairs which was far more terrifying.

For Orwell's main bogey was neither the plan-less chaos of the Great Depression nor the diffusion of American culture, but the imminent triumph of the totalitarian mentality – not so much in Nazi Germany or the Soviet Union, since those were already facts of life, as among the British intelligentsia. 'The scene of the book is laid in Britain,' he wrote in a 1949 statement, 'in order to emphasise that the English-speaking races are not innately better than anyone else and that totalitarianism, *if not fought against*, could triumph anywhere' (see Crick 1980 [1982: 569]). Throughout the 1940s Orwell was preoccupied with what he saw as the intelligentsia's totalitarian leanings and power-worship, and the resulting 'schizophrenia' of those who followed a party line. Another, and related, anxiety was the fading of the concept of 'objective truth' and the disappearance of history – fears which had preoccupied him since his experience of the distortions of propaganda in the Spanish Civil War. By the mid-1940s there was also the emerging international situation to worry about, the dawning age of the superpowers and the Cold War.

ANNA VANINSKAYA

To the extent that Orwell and Huxley were both working within the conventions of a broader dystopian tradition, these divergences could be papered over in the interests of a common anti-Wellsian 'revolt'. A few years after *Brave New World* was published, Orwell suggested as much in his documentary-cum-polemic *The Road to Wigan Pier* (1937):

> [I]t is worth comparing H. G. Wells's *The Sleeper Awakes* with Aldous Huxley's *Brave New World*, written thirty years later. Each is a pessimistic Utopia, a vision of a sort of prig's paradise in which all the dreams of the 'progressive' person come true. ... [Wells] draws a picture of a glittering, strangely sinister world in which the privileged classes live a life of shallow gutless hedonism, and the workers, reduced to a state of utter slavery and sub-human ignorance, toil like troglodytes in caverns underground ... in his more characteristic Utopias ... he returns to optimism and to a vision of humanity, 'liberated' by the machine, as a race of enlightened sunbathers whose sole topic of conversation is their own superiority to their ancestors. *Brave New World* belongs to a later time and to a generation which has seen through the swindle of 'progress' ... it is ... a memorable assault on the more fat-bellied type of perfectionism. Allowing for the exaggerations of caricature, it probably expresses what a majority of thinking people feel about machine-civilisation (*CWGO* 5: 188-189).

The critique of 'machine society' and 'the beehive state', the liberal valorisation of the independent individual in danger of being subsumed by a mass civilisation, of autonomous thought in a world of conformity, do indeed characterise the majority of dystopias written in the first half of the twentieth century. Both Huxley and Orwell fit this mould. Both also portray a society which actively seeks to shape human nature and divides its population into castes along essentially intellectual lines – Orwell's Outer Party are Huxley's Alphas and Betas, the Inner Party are the World Controllers, while the proles are kept in subjection using many of the same means of social (if not biological) engineering as the Bokanovsky clones. Fear and surveillance are reserved for the likes of Winston Smith. For the proles there is mass culture and entertainment: the novel-writing machines in the Fiction Department of the Ministry of Truth on which Julia works, where plots are 'roughed in' on 'big kaleidoscopes' (*CWGO* 9: 111); the 'countless ... songs published for the benefit of the proles by a sub-section of the Music Department' whose words 'were composed without any human intervention whatever on an instrument known as a versificator' (ibid: 144-145). Other amusements include gambling, the lottery, the pub, film and mass spectacle. Both dystopias feature incessant propaganda on page and screen, synthetic music and manufactured 'prolefeed' of various kinds – the television is always on in both books. The predominant note in *Nineteen Eighty-Four* is old-fashioned cockney vulgarity, rather than jazzy Hollywood slickness:

> It was only an 'opeless fancy,
> It passed like an Ipril dye,
> But a look an' a word an' the dreams they stirred
> They 'ave stolen my 'eart awye! (*CWGO* 9: 144).

vs.

> Hug me till you drug me, honey;
> Kiss me till I'm in a coma:
> Hug me, honey, snuggly bunny;
> Love's as good as *soma* (Huxley 1932 [1994: 150]).

But the outcome is the same: enforced ignorance of any alternative mode of existence.

THE NOVELS' GREATEST DIFFERENCE: HOPE AND THE WORKING CLASS

Yet it is within these similarities that the greatest differences reside. For in Orwell's dystopia, hope lies in the proles. They are the ones who manage to stay human, to humanise even the synthetic songs: 'But the woman sang so tunefully as to turn the dreadful rubbish into an almost pleasant sound' (*CWGO* 9: 145). The proles sing, they procreate and they remain sane; while intellectuals like Winston 'are the dead' (ibid: 230). For Huxley, it is the other way around. The belief that Deltas and Epsilons can be liberated is a sign of the Savage's absurdity – the working classes are past recall; if hope there is, it lies in the misfit intellectuals like Helmholtz Watson. The Huxley of *Brave New World* is, ultimately, an elitist. Orwell, for all his inherited class prejudices, is not. He spent his whole writing life praising, glorifying, idealising and romanticising the working classes: they are the 'blind plant struggling towards the light', the 'crystal spirits' of the Spanish Civil War writings, the decent common men who never 'parted company with their moral code', who remain immune to the totalitarian idea that Orwell believed was taking progressively stronger hold of the intellectuals. There is more than a touch of condescension in the idealisation, for the workers are unconscious, not to say stupid: 'The woman down there [who sang the song] had no mind, she had only strong arms, a warm heart, and a fertile belly' (*CWGO* 9: 228). But that warm heart and fertile belly are the key:

> Sooner or later it would happen, strength would change into consciousness. The proles were immortal, you could not doubt it when you looked at that valiant figure in the yard. In the end their awakening would come. And until that happened, though it might be a thousand years, they would stay alive against all the odds, like birds, passing on from body to body the vitality which the Party did not share and could not kill (ibid: 229).

ANNA VANINSKAYA

Huxley's Epsilons are also immortal, but they are infertile. The sexual metaphor – vitality, like semen, passing from body to body – is inoperative in the brave new world, with its freemartins, Malthusian drills and bottled babies. The uniformity of the biologically engineered clones is the rock, the foundation upon which the social stability of the World State rests. In *Nineteen Eighty-Four*, on the contrary, the sameness of the proles, of human beings in other words, is the source of hope:

> It was curious to think that the sky was the same for everybody, in Eurasia or Eastasia as well as here. And the people under the sky were also very much the same – everywhere, all over the world, hundreds of thousands of millions of people just like this, people ignorant of one another's existence, held apart by walls of hatred and lies, and yet almost exactly the same – people who had never learned to think but who were storing up in their hearts and bellies and muscles the power that would one day overturn the world. If there was hope, it lay in the proles! … everywhere stood the same solid unconquerable figure, made monstrous by work and childbearing, toiling from birth to death and still singing. Out of those mighty loins a race of conscious beings must one day come. You were the dead; theirs was the future (*CWGO* 9: 229-230).

Nineteen Eighty-Four is no less ambiguous a book than *Brave New World*. The passage above relays Winston's thoughts using free indirect discourse; in fact, much of the novel is written using third-person limited narration – the favoured narrative perspective of Orwell's fiction. The reader only knows what Winston knows, sees through his eyes and shares in his mistakes. It is possible that he is wrong and O'Brien is right: no evidence is ever adduced, after all, that the proles are capable of awakening. But the possibility is raised and cannot be put back in its box, and this makes *Nineteen Eighty-Four*, for all its grimness, a more hopeful book than *Brave New World*. Both conclude with the defeat of the rebel:

> He loved Big Brother (*CWGO* 9: 311).

> Just under the crown of the arch dangled a pair of feet (Huxley 1932 [1994: 237]).

But ironically, it is the lighter, funnier book that extirpates most completely any hope of a future rebellion. The proles may, perhaps, rise up; we know for a fact that the Epsilons never will.

FURTHER CONTRASTS: SEX, TECHNOLOGY AND WAR

Such differences within similarity may be observed everywhere. The obsession with sex is one telling point of comparison: sexual and emotional energy is released in 'orgy-porgy' rituals of love in *Brave New World*, while in *Nineteen Eighty-Four* it is suppressed and sublimated in the frenzy of the two-minute hate. Social stability is maintained via the dissipation of sexual passion in promiscuity in the former, and via its bottling up in chastity rituals and redirection towards leader-worship and political zealotry in the latter. If Julia is 'a rebel from the waist downwards', as Winston calls her, so is the Savage – but in a diametrically opposing fashion.

Technology is another such point of contrast. Unlike *Brave New World*, which has all the trappings of the pulp sci-fi of the time – the transcontinental rockets, the aluminum hats with wireless transmitters – there is nothing futuristic about the world of *Nineteen Eighty-Four*. All the technologies described, except the surveillance function of the telescreen, were already in existence at the time of writing, and as Goldstein's book makes clear, Oceania is a shabbier, more primitive place than the one Orwell's readers were used to. Both societies proscribe pure science, but Huxley – the grandson, brother, and half-brother of famous evolutionary biologists and eugenicists – builds his dystopia on a scientific basis. Stability is ultimately due to biological engineering; the people are kept amused by technological gadgetry. Orwell's world is, on the contrary, a technologically backward place where 'experiment and invention have largely stopped':

> Science, in the old sense, has almost ceased to exist. … The empirical method of thought, on which all the scientific achievements of the past were founded, is opposed to the most fundamental principles of Ingsoc. And even technological progress only happens when its products can in some way be used for the diminution of human liberty. In all the useful arts the world is either standing still or going backwards (*CWGO* 9: 201).

The Party's control depends upon the destruction 'of the products of human labour' (ibid: 198), and upon a technological stalemate, in the context of an atomic détente, between the three superpowers. Efficiency, security and the mass-production-based and consumer-oriented universal prosperity of *Brave New World* are explicitly the antithesis of what the Party aspires to:

> It was possible, no doubt, to imagine a society in which *wealth*, in the sense of personal possessions and luxuries, should be evenly distributed, while *power* remained in the hands of a small privileged caste. But in practice such a society could not long remain stable. For if leisure and security were enjoyed by all alike, the great mass of human beings who are normally stupefied by poverty would become literate and would learn to think for themselves (*CWGO* 9: 197-198).

Huxley solves the problem of stupefying that great mass by an intricate programme of social conditioning and biological predestination. One cannot help thinking that Orwell's solution – continuous war resulting in chronic *in*security – is more elegant in its simplicity. It was also, in the late 1940s, the much more relevant solution. First-time readers often skip Goldstein's book – the socio-political meat in the thriller sandwich – but Orwell considered this tripartite structure essential. When the Book of the Month Club in America wanted to cut the middle section from their edition, Orwell refused, and the Club had to back down. Goldstein's book contains much of Orwell's thought on international politics, which he had hammered out in numerous essays and reviews in the previous decade. The three super-states that cannot be conquered or overthrown; the role of the atomic bomb as a deterrent; permanent wars by proxy in the third world (a.k.a. the former colonies) and a phony war at home; severance from the outside world and the denial of humanity to the enemy resulting in a hot-house psychological atmosphere; the power-hungry intellectual class using the masses to create a totalitarian society based on slavery with a divine oligarchy at the top; maintenance of inequality by the destruction of the produce of labour; the possibility that such a society might remain static for millennia: Orwell envisioned all this as a real possibility in the 1940s, especially as the Cold War kicked into gear.

THE REALITIES OF TOTALITARIANISM

In fact, none of the distinctive touches of *Nineteen Eighty-Four* were invented by Orwell specially for this book. Purges, frame-ups and mass arrests, spurious confessions, the atmosphere of suspicion and fear, newspapers peddling fantasies and propaganda, the impossibility of producing an objective record, the rewriting of the past: all made their first appearance in his account of the Stalinist hijacking of the Republican cause in *Homage to Catalonia* (1938). Orwell's first novel, the anti-imperialist *Burmese Days* (1934), had already adumbrated the distinction between an Outer Party whose thoughts are censored and who are not free to speak – these were the English functionaries of Empire – and the proles or 'natives' who are left to their own devices, and are only punished physically when they step out of line.

In 'Looking Back on the Spanish War' (1942), 'Notes on Nationalism' (1945), 'The Freedom of the Press' (1945), 'The Prevention of Literature' (1946), 'Politics and the English Language' (1946), 'Second Thoughts on James Burnham' (1946), 'Toward European Unity' (1947) and other essays and articles, Orwell developed the metaphoric significance of $2 + 2 = 5$ and the notion of schizophrenic self-deception that he would later call doublethink. And he bewailed 'indifference to reality', the fading of the notion of objective truth, lies becoming historical fact, and belief in the mutability of the past. He described emotions being turned on and off like a tap; instantaneous switching of sides (literally in mid-sentence) in accordance with the flipping party line; constant changes of policy requiring constant rewritings of history, including document forgery of exactly the same sort as Winston performs on a daily basis; the destruction of language, and language whose purpose is to 'make lies sound truthful and murder respectable, and give an appearance of solidity to pure wind' (*CWGO* 17: 430). He wrote of the blank spectacle stare, 'the gramophone mind' and orgiastic triumph over the enemy. None of these were jottings for his fictional dystopia: all were analyses of actual events, actions and tendencies that he observed around him in the 1930s and 1940s. And the answer he offered to all of them, the desired utopian alternative to this real dystopian world, was always the same: democratic socialism.

When *Nineteen Eighty-Four* was misinterpreted upon its publication as an anti-socialist polemic, Ingsoc identified with the Labour Party, and the whole thing pigeon-holed as the prophecy of a disillusioned left-winger about what would happen if capitalism were not defended, Orwell had to issue press releases insisting that the book was not intended as an attack on socialism. Its purpose was to draw out the logical consequences of the totalitarian ideas that had taken root in the minds of intellectuals who had lost touch with the English tradition of liberty and decency. *Nineteen Eighty-Four*, was, in effect, the wish-fulfilment fantasy of those power-hungry and power-worshiping intellectuals, the managerial class identified by the American political theorist James Burnham, whose books furnished much of the material for Orwell's thinking on totalitarianism. It was the world the pigs of *Animal Farm* would create if they remained in control long enough. The anti-Soviet patina – and there is no doubt that Orwell's dystopia was as anti-Soviet as Huxley's was anti-American: his satire ranged from the obvious (such as modelling Goldstein on Trotsky) to small details such as the cultivation of child spies – this patina was a red herring. What the world of Ingsoc required was *more* socialism, not less.

SOLITUDE AND SOLIDARITY

The fate of Winston Smith illustrates this perfectly. Ultimately, Winston fails because he is alone, because of the individual nature of his revolt. He is aware of this from the start: the end is subsumed in the beginning. He knows that he can never form links with others, that no collective rebellion is possible, and O'Brien confirms this. The hope that may or may not lie in the proles does not apply to him. Winston can only perform a series of individual and, therefore, futile gestures; hopelessness and fatalism are his inevitable portion. The only link he does manage to forge, which gives him strength for the duration of the novel – the link with Julia, the link of love – is precisely the one the Party bends its utmost efforts to destroy.

It is significant that Room 101 is the place where human feelings and human loyalty are betrayed – the feelings and loyalty that the proles maintain despite all odds and that explain why they function as the only carriers of hope and sanity in the dystopian world. The Party wants to substitute love of Big Brother for love of one's fellow human beings, but it can only convert the individual mind – the mind stripped of all attachment to others. Alone, the heretic rebel is powerless, as Winston proves to be; and what O'Brien offers in place of real collectivism is 'collective solipsism' (*CWGO* 9: 279). Reality control by the Party is possible only if reality is in the mind of the individual. Step outside the individual mind, make connections with other human beings on the basis of a shared consensus of the senses, and the Party's power dissipates. This is why the other main site of resistance to totalitarian ideology in *Nineteen Eighty-Four* – other than the proles, that is – is the accurate memory of the past.

The World Controllers in *Brave New World* also prohibit all knowledge of the past as a potential source of discontent, of alternative views that might destabilise the status quo. But Orwell goes far beyond this. The mutability of the past is essential for the Party not just for epistemological but for ontological reasons: not just in order to control records, to appear infallible, but to ensure that every individual exists in an eternal present, in a reality of the Party's making. When everything outside the present moment becomes mist, the mind loses its bearings as the body does 'in interstellar space' where there is 'no way of knowing which direction is up and which is down' (ibid: 207). In the torture scenes, O'Brien's 'insane' Bishop Berkeley-like idealism, the theory that reality exists only in the mind (and in the mind of God, whose role the Party helpfully assumes), is pitched explicitly against Winston's 'sane' empiricism: the data of your senses about the external world, the photograph you and others have seen. Without those, the individual is helpless, hopelessly adrift and unmoored, the 'last man' indeed, as O'Brien calls Winston. Only solidarity, paradoxically, can secure real autonomy. Only other people can help you get your bearings back as an individual.

THE SAD ENDS OF WINSTON AND THE SAVAGE

'Solidarity', of course, is one of the mottos of Huxley's World State. Huxley and Orwell both specialised in coining memorable ironic mottos for their dystopias, but the irony was always double-edged. Loneliness and individualism are the necessary preconditions for rebellion in both books, but they are not sufficient ones. The sad ends of Winston and the Savage, and to a certain extent Bernard Marx, are reminders of that. No other end is possible in a dystopia, for if a way could be found to transcend the loneliness of the dissenter, it would have to be called a utopia instead. To tweak the concluding words of the narrator of William Morris's famous socialist utopia *News from Nowhere* (1891), 'if others [could] see it as I have seen it, then it may be called a vision rather than a [bad] dream' (ibid: 228). Winston's tragedy is that no one will see things as he sees them, no one will help him awake from his bad dream, break out from his third-person limited point of view to achieve meaningful omniscience. True utopian solidarity, unlike the perverted kind enforced by Huxley's and Orwell's dystopian states, involves the voluntary coming together of autonomous individuals,[4] and it is in their negation of this possibility, in their withholding of the 'vision' of social transformation or the redemption of the failed rebel, that *Brave New World* and *Nineteen Eighty-Four* approach each other most intimately despite all their differences.

The main failed rebel of Huxley's dystopia is not, as the narrative first seems to imply, Bernard Marx, but a figure who comes straight out of the nineteenth-century tradition of utopian romance, trailing even older noble savage associations behind him (not to mention contemporary Lawrentian ones). William Morris, again, provides the clearest point of reference. Like Huxley's Savage, the hero of William Morris's 1891 fantasy of a deceptive earthly paradise, *The Story of the Glittering Plain*, arrives in a land of eternal youth, whose beautiful inhabitants live a perfectly happy life of sensual pleasure and sexual fulfilment of a semi-promiscuous kind, and simply cannot understand his preference for hard work, purposeful striving and passionate attachment to one beloved. Again, like the Savage in conversation with Mustapha Mond, Morris's hero, in conversation with the ruler of the Glittering Plain, is offered a rhetorical choice between two worlds: 'Without [the Glittering Plain] is battle and famine, longing unsatisfied, and heart-burning and fear; within it is plenty and peace and good will and pleasure without cease' (op cit: 93).

Like the Savage, Morris's hero chooses danger, freedom, pain and unhappiness, and goes off to live by himself in order to find a way to escape this seeming heaven which is for him a hell. The inhabitants come to watch him at his work, uncomprehending. But John Savage does not, like Morris's stalwart hero, return to the land of his birth, and the New Mexican Reservation he comes from is not the pre-modern but honourable society from which Morris's protagonist hails.

This distinction goes to the heart of Huxley's dystopian project. As he explains in his 1946 Foreword, *Brave New World* offers a picture of two extremes, two opposite forms of lunacy:

> The Savage is offered only two alternatives, an insane life in Utopia, or the life of a primitive in an Indian village, a life more human in some respects, but in others hardly less queer and abnormal. At the time the book was written this idea, that human beings are given free will in order to choose between insanity on the one hand and lunacy on the other, was one that I found amusing and regarded as quite possibly true … at the

close, of course, he is made to retreat from sanity; his native *Penitente*-ism reasserts its authority and he ends in maniacal self-torture and despairing suicide (1932 [1994: xxviii]).

What the Savage's end represents is not an embattled human normality against which to contrast the dehumanised perversions of the brave new world, but a photographic negative of the World State. The fanatically penitential rituals in which he engages, the self-punishment and expiation of guilt, are disproportionate reactions to the society he encounters. They are the pendulum swinging away from the ignorant idealisation with which he began. A similar reversal occurs in the Savage's attitude to Lenina, but neither extreme constitutes a considered rational response, and it is obvious that chaste veneration and Freudian sadomasochism are equally flawed models of behaviour. The Savage's self-flagellation so easily turns into an 'orgy-porgy' at the end of the book precisely because the distance between the two is not as great as it may appear. They are merely obverse sides of the same coin, like the virgin and whore categories that are the only ones available to the Savage in his interactions with Lenina.

The only genuine alternative to the Savage's self-destruction is provided by the off-stage island societies of exiled subversive intellectuals where, it is implied, genuine freedom of thought is possible. There truth and beauty, in Mustapha Mond's words, can be pursued free from the superstitions, cruelties and excesses that characterise the Savage and the Reservation that formed him, and, in a different but related guise, the 'civilised' London that is the Reservation's antithesis. But these societies are sterile, like so much else in the brave new world: they have no social progeny. The Savage fails in the end because he cannot break out of the insane binary into which his world entraps him, Winston because he cannot counter O'Brien's insanity on his own.

CONCLUSION

Regarded as satires or prophecies, *Brave New World* and *Nineteen Eighty-Four* complete each other perfectly. The history of the modern world, whether in Huxley's hedonistic American or Orwell's totalitarian European dress, is a lunatic nightmare from which their doomed protagonists can never awake. However much their visions differed formally and thematically, this shared preoccupation with political and moral insanity is one of the most durable elements that the two dystopian writers bequeathed to subsequent literature. In 1959, Eugène Ionesco's absurdist play *Rhinoceros* transferred the predicament of the 'last man' to the stage in a more starkly allegorical manner than either Huxley or Orwell could allow themselves in their novels. Romantic love – the last bond – fails in the face of monstrous pressure just as it does in *Nineteen Eighty-Four*. And the last human being in the play is left alone, almost succumbing to, but ultimately defying – with nothing but his humanity left to fall back upon – the mustered forces of a 'mad' and inhuman world.

The literary gallery of the second half of the twentieth century and the beginning of the twenty-first is full of such portraits. The backdrops may take their tints alternately from the World State's high-tech prosperity or from Oceania's dilapidated austerity, from the former's permissiveness or the latter's puritanism; the colours may darken to Orwellian terror or lighten to Huxleyan humour; hope may flicker in or out. But the solitary central figure remains constant, poised precariously on the edge, an enduring allegorical personification of the human spirit facing the insane futures human beings have created.

NOTES

[1] Thanks are due to John Rodden for his comments on an earlier version of this essay

[2] Book review published in *Tribune* on 12 July 1940. Orwell would go on to make substantially the same point about the irrelevance of Huxley's 'hedonistic parody of the Wellsian Utopia' in the age of Hitler in numerous publications, including the essay 'Wells, Hitler and the World State' (1941) and the review of Yevgeny Zamyatin's *We*, to which he believed Huxley was indebted, in *Tribune* of 4 January 1946

[3] The epigraph to *Brave New World*, taken from the Russian philosopher Nikolai Berdyaev, asked precisely this question: how do we avoid the realisation of utopias? After the war, in his 1946 Foreword, Huxley asserted that this realisation was much closer than he had imagined fifteen years previously (1932 [1994: xxxvi]), but now he too, like Orwell, dubbed his version of the coming 'utopian' future an insane totalitarianism

[4] See Huxley's 1946 Foreword: 'If I were now to rewrite the book, I would offer the Savage a third alternative … learning something at first hand about the nature of a society composed of freely co-operating individuals devoted to the pursuit of sanity' (1932 [1994: ixxx])

REFERENCES

Crick, Bernard (1980 [1982]) *George Orwell: A Life*, London: Penguin Books

Huxley, Aldous (1932 [1994]) *Brave New World*, London: Flamingo

Morris, William (1891 [1998]) *News from Nowhere and Other Writings*, Wilmer, Clive (ed.) London: Penguin Books

Morris, William (1891 [1927]) *The Story of the Glittering Plain*, London: Longmans, Green and Co.

Orwell, George (1998) *The Complete Works of George Orwell: 20 Vols (CWGO)* Davison, Peter (ed.) London: Secker & Warburg

Smith, Grover (ed.) (1969) *Letters of Aldous Huxley*, New York: Harper and Row

NOTE ON THE CONTRIBUTOR

Anna Vaninskaya is a Senior Lecturer in Victorian Literature at the University of Edinburgh. She is the author of *William Morris and the Idea of Community: Romance, History and Propaganda, 1880-1914* (Edinburgh UP, 2010), as well as over forty articles and book chapters and several journal special issues on

ANNA VANINSKAYA topics ranging from nineteenth-century socialism, education, popular reading and historical cultures to speculative and fantasy fiction and Anglo-Russian cultural relations. She has taught Orwell for many years, and has published essays on Orwell's socialism, reception history and realist novels.

PAPER

'Such, Such Were the Joys' and the Journalistic Imagination

RICHARD LANCE KEEBLE

Much of the debate over Orwell's essay 'Such, Such Were the Joys', about his years at St Cyprian's prep school, concentrates on the extent to which his recollections are truthful or imagined. Little attention has been directed at the literary elements of the essay. This paper examines in detail the literary devices Orwell uses: such as dramatic narratives, verbatim dialogue, the balancing of tones and attitudes, the sexually explicit, the polemical, confessional and intimate voices, historical generalisations, the journalistic style and social/cultural analysis. Orwell also uses the memoir to explore a vast range of issues: personal identify, fact, fiction, education, sexuality, morality, religion, education and private education in particular, the psychology of children, the baffling incomprehensibility of the world to the child's mind. In addition, it explores such issues as the importance of the critical, historical imagination, literary genres, the need to confound expectations and speak the unspeakable, memory, polemic, self-revelation and the powers of the reflective mind. Above all, the paper examines the complexities of Orwell's seemingly 'plain style'.

Keywords: 'Such, Such Were the Joys', journalistic imagination, truth, fiction

BEYOND THE FACT/FICTION BINARY

Much of the debate over Orwell's long, 15,000-word essay 'Such, Such Were the Joys', about his years (1911-1917) at St Cyprian's prep school near Eastbourne, East Sussex, concentrates on the extent to which Orwell's memoir is truthful or imagined. As Peter Marks summarises (2011: 185), Orwell (or Eric Blair as he was then) finds himself 'regularly in a state of apprehension and abasement: humiliated by the headmaster and (especially) the headmaster's wife, nicknamed Sambo and Flip respectively, degraded by teachers; bullied and sneered at by those of a supposedly superior class; forced to endure mindless teaching, physical privations and filth'.

RICHARD LANCE KEEBLE

Significantly, biographer D. J. Taylor (2003) concludes: 'A trawl through the reminiscences of several old boys supplies evidence to rebut, or at any rate to call into serious question, nearly all of Orwell's allegations. Far from being a sadistic flogger, Mr Wilkes was remembered as a shy and notably unaggressive character. … As for the supposed squalor of the school, this, for nearly half the duration of Eric's stay, was the Great War, when food was scarce and comfort at a premium.'

On the other hand, refuting this, Gordon Bowker (2003: 29) quotes Cecil Beaton, a contemporary at St Cyprian's, suggesting that Orwell had, despite some exaggeration, 'seen through all the layers of snobbery and pretence' of the couple who ran it and 'captured them both perfectly'.

Yet this approach tends to miss the essential purpose of the essay – which was to raise serious questions through various literary devices (which have gone largely unexplored) about a vast range of subjects: personal identify, fact, fiction, education, sexuality, morality, religion, education and private education in particular, the psychology of children, the baffling incomprehensibility of the world to the child's mind. In addition, it explores such issues as the importance of the critical, historical imagination, literary genres, the need to confound expectations and speak the unspeakable, the unreliability of memory, self-revelation and the powers of the reflective mind. Jeffrey Meyers (2000: 17) describes it as 'a masterpiece of polemical autobiography … one of the best essays in English'.

Alex Woloch (2016: 54) highlights Orwell's 'persistent confusion of fiction and nonfiction' and argues that the 'nonfictional' text 'is always in danger of being most deceptive (because we take it too easily at face value)'. In a similar mode, Orwell's biographer Bernard Crick (1980: 35) usefully comments that 'Such, Such' is 'the most puzzling of all his works to locate accurately between fiction and non-fiction'.

> Do we think of documentaries as necessarily conveying the literal truth about the 'I' who pretends to be what the author must know he never can be, 'a camera'? Should we rather not try to gain some critical distance from the documentary technique by exploring the author's intentions biographically as well as by examining the literary result (ibid).

This paper, following Crick, will attempt to identify the literary elements which make it so 'brilliant' (ibid).

THE COMPLEXITY OF ORWELL'S PLAIN STYLE

Orwell is famous for his clear prose, his 'plain style' (Woloch 2016). At the end of his essay, 'Why I Write' (1946 [1970: 30]), he summed up this approach this way: 'Good prose is like a window pane.' But contradictions/complexities/paradoxes even accompany this seemingly clear statement. It comes after he has written: '…yet it is also true that one can write nothing readable unless one constantly struggles to efface one's own personality.' In a sense, all of Orwell's writing (his novels, non-fiction, essays, poetry, journalism) is autobiographical in that it is overtly drawing from his own subjective experiences and political/ethical/literary preoccupations. As Gordon Bowker comments astutely (2003: 145): 'The autobiographical element was a means by which he tried always to relate what he wrote to his own life, continually to reveal himself within the mental landscape through which he was passing. It lent his writing a quality of pilgrimage.'

Lynette Hunter (1984: 1) is right, then, to stress the complexity of his literary strategy. She comments:

> From the beginning he recognizes that the distinction between form and content, subject and object, fiction and documentary, are all versions of the fundamental separation between fact and value that has dominated rationalist humanism since the seventeenth century. And for Orwell, the final question is indeed one of value and morality; his writing career is concerned with a search for a valid voice with which to persuade others and express opinion.

Indeed, for Woloch (2016: 44), Orwell's plain style 'always expresses the *hope* that an idea will come across directly, fully actualized in one specific event of writing. But Orwell's prodigious, formally shifting work sweeps up all such actualized moments into a much larger, and thus less finalized, textual field' (italics in the original).

Most literature is written with a clear audience in mind, and, in some respects, this can serve as a constraint on the creative process. Orwell, in contrast, composed 'Such, Such' with no real expectation of it ever being published in his lifetime. It libelled the headmaster and his wife – and, as he acknowledged, it was too long for a periodical (*CWGO* 19: 149). Alex Woloch (2016: 330) describes it as 'an intentionally posthumous publication'. As a result, it seems a feeling of intense creative freedom propels the writing throughout.

If Orwell did have any sense of an 'imaginary audience' it would have been his friend Cyril Connolly who was at the school when Blair arrived and who would later, as editor of *Horizon*, publish many of Orwell's most celebrated essays. Significantly, his *Enemies of Promise* (1938 [1961]) carries an autobiographical section, 'A Georgian Boyhood', in which he remembers his time at St Cyprian's (called St Wulfric's – also to avoid any libel hassles) somewhat more approvingly than Orwell. He even describes Flip as a 'warm-hearted

RICHARD LANCE KEEBLE

and inspired teacher' (ibid: 174). Orwell may well have conceived 'Such, Such Were the Joys' as a riposte to Connolly. Yet, in *Enemies*, Orwell is mentioned by name – and very positively:

> I was a stage rebel, Orwell a true one. Tall, pale, with his flaccid cheeks, large spatulate fingers and supercilious voice, he was one of those boys who seem born old. ... He saw through St Wulfric's, despised Sambo and hated Flip but was invaluable to them as scholarship fodder. ... The remarkable thing about Orwell was that alone among the boys he was intellectual and not a parrot for he thought for himself, read Shaw and Samuel Butler and rejected not only St Wulfric's but the war, the Empire, Kipling, Sussex and Character (ibid: 178; 179).

Jeremy Lewis, in his biography of Connolly (1998: 95), records how Orwell, in his earlier essay on the British intelligentsia, 'Inside the Whale' (1940), had referred, 'somewhat scathingly', to the 'Theory of Permanent Adolescent' and continued:

> Cultured middle class life has reached a depth of softness at which a public school education – five years in a lukewarm bath of snobbery – can actually be looked upon as an eventful period. To nearly all the writers who have counted during the thirties, what more has ever happened than Mr Connolly records in *Enemies of Promise*? It is the same pattern all the time: public school, university, a few trips abroad, then London. Hunger, hardship, solitude, exile, war, prison, persecution, manual labour – hardly ever words (ibid).

By the late 1940s, Orwell's views about the centrality of boyhood experiences to the formation of character had changed dramatically – and in 'Such, Such' he put the record straight. At the same time, he noticeably failed to celebrate any friendship with a fellow pupil (either Connolly or any other) at St Cyrprian's. Daphne Patai comments (1984: 7): 'As a writer, Orwell was primarily stimulated by negative impulses: he needed to write *against* something' (italics in the original).

THE TITLE AND SECTION I: GENDER POLITICS AND LITERARY JOURNALISM

The threat of being beaten

The title itself indicates that this is going to be a deliberately constructed literary/creative work. It is taken from 'The Echoing Green', one of Blake's *Songs of Innocence* poems (of 1789). Bowker comments (2003: 66): 'As the mature Orwell fully realized, an echoing green is a more complex metaphor for the relationship between artistic and literal truth. ... If he mocked myths of childhood joy unbounded, he was surely well aware that by using such a quotation as the title of his essay he was drawing attention to the fact that the author was the creator, not remembrancer. Echoes both repeat and distort.' The opening tone is ironic; and the essential message is: 'Don' take this as the literal truth.'

Interestingly, the essay is divided into six sections. It was clearly a structure that appealed to Orwell: his study of Dickens (1939) was similarly divided. The strategy serves a number of important purposes: each section, we can assume as readers, carries distinct ideas and themes; it helps the reading process by providing breaks (reading 'breathing spaces') through what otherwise would have been an intimidating 15,000 words; and at the start of each section, the text assumes a new energy, a new rhythmic vitality, a new significance. In some respects this is drawing on the conventions of journalism in which various strategies are adopted (e.g. the insertion of space in the copy followed by a few words in capital letters, say) to indicate thematic changes and introduce rhythmic variety into the copy.

The most obvious feature of journalistic writing is the stress on the most important or the most dramatic in the opening section (known, in the jargon, as the 'intro'). This convention only emerged after decades of newspaper writing, driven largely by commercial imperatives and the need for concise writing (newspaper space, in effect, costing money). Distinguishing itself from fiction in the crowded marketplace of ideas, journalism succeeded on the basis of its claims to accuracy and authenticity with the most important and dramatic 'facts' being thrust at the top of stories to draw the attention of the reader (Keeble 2007: 9). Here, Orwell, in effect, gives play to his 'journalistic imagination', beginning with a particularly striking, shocking, highly personalised, confessional narrative ('I' appears six times in the first three sentences).

The writing, as in journalism, is concise. The sentences are short. He begins: 'Soon after I arrived at St Cyprian's (not immediately, but after a week or two, just when I seemed to be settling into the routine of school life) I began wetting my bed.' The words in the parenthesis delay slightly the full impact of the revelation but when it appears at the end of the sentence ('I began wetting my bed.') it carries all the more weight. Perhaps in no other way could Eric Blair (as Orwell then was) more offend the manly ethos of the school than through this overt display of effeminacy: as in the second par, Orwell writes: '… it was looked on as a disgusting crime which the child committed on purpose and for which the proper cure was a beating' (1952 [1970: 379]). The opening dramatic narrative then moves through a series of happenings which culminate (inevitably) in a beating for Blair.

Intriguingly, the manly ethos is enforced in the first instance by two women: indeed, the tensions surrounding gender and sexuality are

RICHARD LANCE KEEBLE

to run through the text. We are first introduced to Mrs W., the headmaster's wife (her real name, Cicely Wilkes, obscured to avoid libel), only very briefly: originally attention is focused on the lady she is chatting with: 'She was an intimidating, masculine-looking person wearing a riding habit, or something I took to be a riding habit' (ibid). The description of Mrs W. is slightly delayed – so when it does appear it carries more impact. She is nicknamed Flip: there is a lightness and a certain sexual daring about the name – chosen because of her 'flippy-floppy bosom', according to John Sutherland (2016: 61). There is even a warm intimacy in her official name, Mum, that also contrasts with the heaviness of the threat she poses for Blair. Like the other lady, she is described as rather manly: 'She was a stocky square-built woman with hard red cheeks, a flat top to her head, prominent brows and deep-set, suspicious eyes.'

Orwell cleverly conveys the impressions of a sensitive boy alongside the insights of the elderly man looking back on the past.[1] Continuing the manly theme and ever aware of people's speech patterns and rhythms, here Mrs W. is described as 'jollying one along with mannish slang ("Buck up, old chap! And so forth")'. But the elderly narrator, looking back, sees all the 'false heartiness' behind the 'jollying' (1952 [1970: 320]). 'It was very difficult to look her in the face without feeling guilty, even at moments when one was not guilty of anything in particular' (ibid). So this early section of the essay culminates with Flip shaming Blair in front of the stranger by revealing how he 'wets his bed every night' and threatening to get the Sixth Form to beat him if he wets again. Along with guilt and shame comes terror and the freezing of the senses: 'I could not speak.' He mis-hears the phrase 'the Sixth Form' as 'Mrs Form' and assumes this is the strange lady who is to do the beating.

The beating: The fiction/non-fiction continuum
From focusing on the nightmarish fear of being beaten by a strange woman in the essay's opening, the narrative in the second part of the first section culminates in an actual beating – by a man. It begins with a woman, the 'grim statuesque matron', one morning pulling back his bed clothes to reveal the clammy sheets. Orwell captures the terror evoked by her thunderous order by capitalising the first two words of the phrase: 'REPORT YOURSELF to the headmaster after breakfast.' And by making that short sentence a single paragraph, Orwell is using all the literary devices available to highlight the 'dreaded words' (ibid: 381).

Compared to the women involved in the drama – all of whom are described in manly, menacing terms – the man who is to administer the beating (the headmaster, Lewis Chitty Vaughan Wilkes, nicknamed Sambo) is portrayed in precisely the opposite way: he is 'curiously oafish' 'with a chubby face which was like that of an overgrown baby, and which was capable of good humour'. Indeed, throughout the essay Orwell is concerned to show the complex gender politics at play: here the women's violence is manifested in their looks and spiteful words; the man may be a grown up baby but he does the violent deed. Since the beating culminates this part of the essay, Orwell describes it in some detail. Blair begins by admitting his offence:

> When I had said my say, he read me a short but pompous lecture, then seized me by the scruff of the neck, twisted me over and began beating me with the riding crop. He had a habit of continuing his lecture while he flogged you, and I remember the words 'you dir-ty lit-tle boy' keeping time with the blows (ibid).

The tension at the heart of the narrative slackens a little when Blair reports that the beating did not hurt. This was 'a sort of victory and partially wiped out the shame of the bed-wetting'. Some boys are hanging about in the passage outside and a section of dialogue follows:

> 'D'you get the cane?'
> 'It didn't hurt,' I said proudly.
> Flip had heard everything. Instantly her voice came screaming after me:
> 'Come here! Come here this instant! What was that you said?'
> 'I said it didn't hurt,' I faltered out.
> 'How dare you say a thing like that? Do you think that is a proper thing to say? Go in and REPORT YOURSELF AGAIN!' (ibid: 382).

From a literary point of view this (apparently verbatim) dialogue is intriguing. It is tied up with all the other detail of the narrative: it is, in part, a rhetorical strategy to convince the reader of its authenticity and 'truthfulness' (just as the use of direct speech in journalism serves to support its claims for veracity). Trust is crucial in the relationship between the author of non-fiction and the reader: how can we be assured that these are the 'facts' and not fiction? Here, the detail of the remembered dialogue is aiming to convince us of the narrative's truthfulness. As Marks comments (2011: 186): 'The relatively long account gathers some of its persuasive power simply from the quantity of detail supplied, itself a tactic Orwell uses to substantiate the veracity of his testimony.' Yet, paradoxically, that very detail tempts us to doubt its 'truthfulness'. For how can anyone remember events from so long ago with such clarity and in such detail? It must be mainly fiction. Orwell, thus, is deliberately placing his narrative in the space between non-fiction and fiction. As Lynette Hunter (1984: 5) comments on Orwell's experiments with genre:

RICHARD LANCE KEEBLE

...commentators come to the writing with critical expectations that lie within the framework that Orwell came to challenge. The most common expectation is that fiction and non-fiction, the novel and the documentary are always significantly divided from each other and this prevents the reader from appreciating Orwell's own suggestion that they can be viewed fruitfully as part of a continuum.

The drama continues as Sambo lays into Blair, seemingly for about five minutes, ending up breaking the riding crop. 'The bone handle went flying across the room' (ibid). As John Sutherland comments (2016: 64), this final whipping 'has something orgasmic about it – a lachrymose, and unusual, ejaculation of a kind'. Sambo certainly ends up sounding totally absurd, pathetically blaming Blair:

> 'Look what you've made me do!' he said furiously, holding up the broken crop.

Reflections on the Beating

In the final part of the first section, Orwell reflects back on the ordeal – both from a personal perspective and more generally. He cries – and the feelings are complex, extremely powerful, multi-layered and difficult to capture.

> I was crying partly because I felt this was expected of me, partly from genuine repentance, but partly also because of a deeper grief which is peculiar to childhood and not easy to convey: a sense of desolate loneliness and helplessness, of being locked up not only in a hostile world but in a world of good and evil where the rules were such that it was actually not possible for me to keep them (ibid).

It's not surprising the outburst of crying is examined in such detail: after all, like bed-wetting, it was considered sissy and effeminate: an act that was completely out of keeping with the public school ethos of manly service for the empire (see Grant 2004).

A number of commentators have also seen links between the depiction of young Blair in the desolate, lonely and oppressive world of St Cyprian's and the fate of anti-hero Winston Smith in the grim, dystopian novel, *Nineteen Eighty-Four* (1949) which Orwell was working on at the same time. As Bowker argues (2003: 29):

> Orwell's notorious memoir of the school, 'Such, Such Were the Joys', the product of over thirty years of brooding, is his own anatomy of melancholy, complemented only by *Nineteen Eighty-Four*. It is the recollection of a place and period viewed through a highly sensitive and complex mind, filtered through time and coloured by ideology, the account of a closed and oppressive world from the alter ego of Winston Smith, the last apostle of

free thought. It is as much a polemic aimed at the English private school system as a piece of reflective self-analysis…

As Orwell continues his self-analysis, he looks back on the experience with the benefit of hindsight. He remains determined to convince the reader of the authenticity of the account – but, at the same time, to surprise with his conclusions. He moves away from the subjective 'I' voice to comment more generally: '… it can also happen that one's memories grow sharper after a long lapse of time, because one is looking at the past with fresh eyes and can isolate and, as it were, notice facts which previously existed undifferentiated among a mass of others' (1952 [1970: 383). He goes on to conclude, surprisingly, that 'the second beating seemed to me a just and reasonable punishment'. 'To get one beating, and then to get another and far fiercer on top of it, for being so unwise as to show that the first had not hurt – that was quite natural.' And from reflecting with the benefit of hindsight, he is suddenly able to capture more sharply a feeling he experienced at the time of the flogging; 'I accepted the broken riding crop as my own crime' (ibid).

Just as the section structure gives Orwell the opportunity to vary the intensity of the narrative: to open with a focus on intense drama and feelings and move on to calmer reflections so it allows him to end with a striking flourish. Here, Orwell completely confounds expectations. Having stressed the horror of the flogging, he writes:

> I did not wet my bed again – at least, I did wet it once again, and received another beating, after which the trouble stopped. So perhaps this barbarous remedy does work, though at a heavy price, I have no doubt (ibid: 383-384).

D. J. Taylor (2003: 31) comments: 'There are one or two passages in "Such, Such Were the Joys" that indicate a striving for balance' and this may be one such example. But perhaps it is more typical of Orwell the controversialist, the maverick, the writer reflecting critically on his society and on his own experiences. Orwell the man was also constantly changing – both his styles of living (from Eton, to Imperial Police service in Burma, then down and out with the destitute in Paris and London; then teacher, freelance writer, Republican fighter in Spain, broadcaster, literary editor, war correspondent, through all of this a voracious reader) and styles of writing (essayist, novelist, polemicist, poet). Significantly, in his essay 'Why I Write' (1946 [1970: 29]), he commented: 'I find that by the time you have perfected any style of writing, you have outgrown it.' Just as his life was full of surprising turns, so his writing incorporated surprising twists: while the essay appears to be a damning critique of the public school system Orwell slips in reflections which cleverly modify that extreme view.

RICHARD LANCE KEEBLE

SECTION II: FROM THE PERSONAL TO THE POLITICAL

The School as Symbol

Following the intensely personal, dramatic narrative that fills the whole of Section I, in contrast, Section II is more reflective: the focus shifts from the personal to the social, cultural and political. The school – with its hierarchical organisation, the favouritism shown the sons of the wealthy, its obsession with the 'evil' of competition and success and, above all, its 'outrageous' sense of history (and lack of critical awareness of the imperial past) – is shown as a microcosm of the broader society beyond its walls:

> History was a series of unrelated, unintelligible but – in some way that was never explained to us – important facts with resounding phrases tied to them. Disraeli brought peace with honour. Clive was astonished at his moderation (ibid: 386).

History is, then, reduced to mere banal clichés.

The issue of corporal punishment returns – but this time the focus shifts away from the angst-ridden personal drama with the students, in general, shown as passive in the face of the school's bullying regime: 'Indeed, I doubt whether classical education ever has been or can be successfully carried on without corporal punishment. The boys themselves believed in its efficacy' (1952 [1970: 388]). The 'three castes' at the school are shown as reflecting the class divisions in the broader society, and significantly, Orwell identifies with the 'underlings'.

> There was the minority with an aristocratic or millionaire background, there were the children of the ordinary suburban rich, who made up the bulk of the school, and there were a few underlings like myself, the sons of clergymen, Indian civil servants, struggling widows and the like. These poorer ones were discouraged from going in for 'extras' such as shooting and carpentry, and were humiliated over clothes and petty possessions (ibid).

Orwell, in his writings, constantly confronts the difficulty of writing. As he put it in 'Why I Write': 'The job is to reconcile my ingrained likes and dislikes with the essentially public, non-individual activities that this age forces upon all of us. It is not easy. It raises problems of construction and of language and it raises in a new way the problem of truthfulness' (op cit: 28). Earlier in 'Such, Such', he had written of 'the deeper grief which is peculiar to childhood and not easy to convey' (1952 [1970, 4: 382]). Here he again confronts the problem of capturing feelings from so many years ago – which are both highly intense and ambivalent. He says:

> It is not easy to convey to a grown-up person the sense of strain, of nerving oneself for some terrible, all-deciding combat, as the date of the examination crept nearer – eleven years old, twelve years old, then thirteen, the fatal year itself! (ibid: 390).

Clearly central here is the unspoken fear of failure. But the fear is followed 'by an almost irresistible impulse *not* to work' (ibid; italics in the original) so making failure difficult to avoid and so self-inflicted. Throughout his life, Orwell both feared and embraced failure as an important, intrinsic part of human existence (Keeble 2012: 6). Failure is commonly experienced by characters in his novels; and it is a subject for reflection in his nonfiction. So typically he comments in 'Why I Write' (op cit: 29): '…every book is a failure,' Failure (and its opposite, success) was also the subject of a lengthy discussion in Connolly's *Enemies of Promise*. For instance, he writes (1938 [1961: 129]): 'Of all the enemies of literature, success is the most insidious.' To some extent, then, Orwell used 'Such, Such' to continue his dialogue with Connolly about literature and the social standing of authors.

Poverty and St Cyprian's Big Brother

Poverty is another constant Orwellian preoccupation. His first published book *Down and Out in Paris and London* (1933) was his part memoir/part fictional account of his time with the tramps in London and Essex and the Parisian proletariat, *The Road to Wigan Pier* (1937) was his eye-witness, sociological investigation into poverty in Northern England – and so on. 'Probably the greatest cruelty one can inflict on a child is to send it to a school among children richer than itself,' says Gordon Comstock in his novel, *Keep the Aspidistra Flying* (1936). Here, the obsession with poverty focuses on his own, painful predicament which ties in with his fear of being constantly under surveillance. The annual fees of £180 were way beyond the Blairs' means since the salary of his father, an official in the Opium Department of the Indian Civil Service, was just £650 p.a., falling to less than £200 when he retired in 1912. But, as John Sutherland records (2016: 62), Ida, Orwell's mother 'wangled half-fees for Eric'. 'She was helped by the fact that her brother Charles Limouzin lived in Eastbourne and, a hero on the local links, played golf with Lewis, captain of the club.' But Orwell writes:

> I did not at first understand that I was being taken at reduced fees: it was only when I was about eleven that Flip and Sambo began throwing the fact in my teeth. … Sambo, who did not aspire to be loved by his pupils, put it more brutally, though, as was usual with him in pompous language. 'You are living on my bounty' was his favourite phrase in this context (Orwell 1952 [1970, 4: 392]).

Next, to illustrate the pain of poverty, he tells the story of when he secretly went to a sweet shop a mile or more from the school to buy some chocolates. Opposite he sees a 'small sharp-faced man' (ibid). 'Instantly, a horrible fear went through me. There could be no doubt as to who the man was. He was a spy placed there by Sambo!' (ibid). Afterwards, he fears a summons to the head's office – but it never comes. The implication is that young Blair may well have imagined the 'spy'. He continues: 'It did not seem to me strange that the headmaster of a private school should dispose of an army of informers, and I did not even imagine that he would have to pay them. … Sambo was all powerful: it was natural that his agents should be everywhere' (ibid: 392-393). Is Orwell here playing with the notion of the surveillance state dominated by an all-powerful Big Brother which he most creatively realised in his dystopian novel *Nineteen Eighty-Four* (1949)?

The second section comes to a climax with a detailed exploration of his feelings towards St Cyprian's own Big Brother and Big Sister: hate, guilt and shame are all mixed up in the young Blair. He conveys the intensity of the hatred by mentioning it twice: 'I hated Sambo and Flip with a sort of shamefaced remorseful hatred…' and later in the paragraph: 'I hated both of them. I could not control my subjective feeling and I could not conceal them from myself' (ibid). Perhaps worst of all is the sense of helplessness in the face of feelings he could not control. Orwell's whole career as an engaged intellectual, after all, was dedicated to understanding the personal and the political and thereby gain some degree of self-control and power to effect meaningful, progressive change in society.

SECTION III: UNSETTLING THE READER WITH CHANGING MOODS AND ATTITUDES

Part One: Oh the Joy of Those Occasional Expeditions!

This section is extraordinary for the way in which Orwell confounds expectations, constantly unsettling the reader with his changing moods and attitudes. He begins dramatically: 'No one can look back on his schooldays and say with truth that they were altogether unhappy' (ibid: 394). The sentence stands alone as a single paragraph so visually acquiring more impact. Having so far concentrated on the gloom, despair, fear and shame of his St Cyprian's ordeal, he now suddenly shifts tack and remembers some 'good memories … among a horde of bad ones' (ibid). The next paragraph is bursting with positive words: 'wonderful', 'more wonderful', 'joy', 'pleasure', 'excitement' and 'fascinating'. Given the title of the essay, 'joy' is a particularly significant word and the writing appears to reach some kind of climax in the next paragraph when he remembers going butterfly-hunting with a teacher called Brown (presumably a pseudonym): 'and oh, the joy of those occasional expeditions!' (ibid: 395).

But such a positive mood cannot be sustained for long and so the attention quickly shifts back to Flip: 'From her point of view, natural history ("bug-hunting" she would probably have called it) was a babyish pursuit which a boy should be laughed out of as early as possible' (ibid). In other words, an interest in nature was not consistent with the aggressively masculinist ethos of the school – and so had to be mocked. Then the mood suddenly shifts again (even in the same paragraph) with the focus fixed on the teacher Brown. With an awareness of the complex dynamics of working relationships perhaps exceptional for a young boy, Blair sees that Brown, having been at the school from its early days, had built up a certain independence: 'If it ever happened that both of them [Flip and Sambo] were away, Brown acted as deputy headmaster, and on those occasions instead of reading the appointed lesson for the day at morning chapel, he would read us stories from the Apocrypha' (ibid).

The moods in the next paragraph constantly shift, too. For the adult Orwell looking back at the young Blair there appears to be some sort of conclusive finality about this opening short sentence: 'Most of the good memories of my childhood, and up to the age of about twenty, are in some way connected with animals' (ibid: 395-396). And he repeats that phrase 'good memories' in the follow-up sentence, 'goodness' being associated with warmth: 'So far as St Cyprian's goes, it also seems, when I look back, that all my good memories are of summer' (ibid: 396). But the summer joys cannot be sustained and immediately Orwell shifts to bad memories of cold winters: running nose, the daily nightmare of football and the torment of being blamed for his poor health.

Oh, the Squalor!
The rest of this section is devoted to a meticulous and highly detailed examination of the squalid conditions at the school. The writing is clearly fired by anger, hatred and disgust: at the same time, it's always colourful and highly literary. Orwell was throughout his life a voracious reader. Earlier in the essay, he had written: 'Ian Hay, Thackeray, Kipling and H. G. Wells were the favourite authors of my boyhood' (ibid: 394). Here, he deliberately places his depiction of the squalor in a literary context referring (subtly, in passing) to Thackeray, Dickens and Samuel Butler.

The poet and novelist William Makepeace Thackeray (1811-1863) had attended Charterhouse School but had hated it, later dubbing it in his fiction 'Slaughter House'.[2] Here, Orwell writes: 'Almost as in the days of Thackeray, it seemed natural that a little boy of eight or ten should be miserable, snotty-nosed creature, his face almost permanently dirty, his hands chapped, his nails bitten, his handkerchief a sodden horror, his bottom frequently blue with bruises' (ibid: 396). To what extent is Orwell exaggerating? We will never know. But he clearly suspected readers may think so – and so he cleverly disarms this criticism with this reflection: 'Whoever writes about his childhood must beware of exaggeration and self pity' (ibid: 398). He continues, referencing the infamous school of Mr Wackford Squeers, in Dickens's *Nicholas Nickleby* (1839), where pupils are abused and neglected and where Nickleby goes to teach: 'I do not claim that I was a martyr or that St Cyprian's was a sort of Dotheboys Hall. But I should be falsifying my own memories if I did not record that they are largely memories of disgust' (ibid).

The reference to Samuel Butler (1835-1902) is fascinating. His *Erewhon* (of 1872) is an anti-utopian novel, 'part science-fiction, part social commentary, part adventure fantasy, part comic satire' which may well have influenced *Orwell's Nineteen Eighty-Four*.[3] Here, Orwell writes: 'Boys are Erewhonians: they think that misfortune is disgraceful and must be concealed at all costs' (ibid: 400). But perhaps more influential on the Orwell of 'Such, Such Were the Joys' was Butler's subtle representation of Erewhon, always avoiding blanket denunciations. As Tierle comments:

> Butler presents each aspect and institution in the novel from two angles, even while satirising the university (as the Colleges of Unreason) and the church (the worship of 'Mrs Grundy' in the form of Ydgrun). It's always weighed up from two sides. Thus *Erewhon* is strictly speaking, we might say, neither a utopia nor a dystopia but rather what we might call an *equitopia*, a world that is weighed in the balance and neither painted as a nightmare hell-on-earth (or elsewhere) nor depicted as a heavenly paradise.[4]

Food, Glorious Food!

Orwell's disgust first focuses on the meals: 'The food was not only bad, it was also insufficient' (ibid: 397). By the late 1940s, Orwell had developed a heightened awareness of the political/economic factors influencing the individual's psychology – politics, culture, the media and social institutions in general – and had come to see the school essentially as a commercial enterprise dedicated to snobbery. So looking back with the benefit of hindsight, he is able to write: 'As usual, I did not see the sound commercial reason for this underfeeding. On the whole, I accepted Sambo's view that a boy's appetite is a sort of morbid growth which should be kept in check as much as possible' (ibid).

Next, Orwell evokes the horrors of toilet facilities describing 'the slimy water of the plunge bath' and the murky seawater of the local baths which came straight in from the beach and 'on which I once saw floating a human turd' (ibid). He continues: 'It is not easy for me to think of my schooldays without seeming to breathe in a whiff of something cold and evil-smelling – a sort of compound of sweaty stockings, dirty towels, faecal smells blowing along corridors, forks with old food between the prongs, neck-of-mutton stew, and the banging of doors of the lavatories and the echoing chamber-pots in the dormitories' (ibid: 398-399). To a certain extent, the picture drawn here is reminiscent of Orwell's account of his time spent in a spike (1931 [1970: 59-60):

> It was a disgusting sight, that bathroom. All the indecent secrets of our underwear were exposed: the grime, the rents and patches, the bits of string doing duty for buttons, the layers upon layers of fragmentary garments, some of them mere collections of holes, held together by dirt. The room became a press of steaming nudity, the sweaty odours of the tramps competing with the sickly, sub-faecal stench native to the spike.

Paradoxically, then, Orwell's prep school ordeals did not result in a life-long aversion to grime, rather the reverse: for four years, having returned from serving with the Indian Imperial Police in Burma in 1927, he determined to become a writer and voluntarily spent many months with the down and outs. After all, grime, the stench of the spikes and poverty, as he realised, could make great copy…

Flip the Focus, Again

For the final part of this section, Orwell focuses once again on Fiip. In keeping with the overall approach of this section, even here Orwell moderates his animosity: 'Thus, although my memories of Flip are mostly hostile, I also remember considerable periods when I basked under her smiles, when she called me "old chap" and used my Christian name, and allowed me to frequent her private library, where I first made acquaintance with *Vanity Fair*' (1952 [1970, 4: 401). Significantly, reading - in this case Thackeray's celebrated novel of 1848 – is associated for Orwell with positive experiences. And it's Flip's special 'vocabulary of praise and abuse' which particularly draws his attention, Orwell carefully showing the syllables she emphasised through the use of italics:

> There was '*Buck* up, old chap!' which inspired one to paroxysms of energy; there was 'Don't *be* such a fool!' (or, It's pat*hetic*, isn't it), which made one feel a born idiot; and there was 'It isn't very straight of you, isn't it?' which always brought me to the brink of tears (ibid: 402).

The section ends on a powerful, emotional note. But instead of using the 'I' voice he distances himself slightly from the feeling (in keeping with the overall nuanced approach of this section) and talks of the impersonal 'one':

> And yet all the while, at the middle of one's heart, there seemed to stand an incorruptible inner self who knew that whatever one did – whether one laughed or snivelled or went into frenzies of

gratitude for small favour – one only true feeling was hatred (ibid).

SECTION IV: CONFRONTING TABOOS

Sex and homosexuality

Connolly had devoted a whole chapter in *Enemies of Promise* (no. 14: 'The Charlock's Shade') to homosexuality amongst writers but in his chapter on his time at St Wulfric's there was no explicit mention of it. Significantly, the gay writer John Addington Symonds (1840-1893) had written about homosexuality during his time at Harrow – and an affair between a headmaster and pupil, no less – in his autobiography, *Memoirs*. But it was never to be published until 1984.[5] Orwell was clearly determined to confront the taboo – and explore his own sexuality in the process.

This was not first time Orwell had confronted homosexuality in his writings. For instance, even in his first published book, *Down and Out in Paris and London* (1933 [1980]), another complex mix of actuality and fiction (Bowker 3003: 144), he tells of the occasion when he is the victim of a homosexual assault in a spike: 'About midnight the other man began making homosexual attempts on me – a nasty experience in a locked, pitch-dark cell. He was a feeble creature and I could manage him easily, but of course it was impossible to go to sleep again' (1933 [1980]: 86). In the reflective section at the end of the book, he does not condemn but understands the prevalence of homosexuality amongst tramps in the context of the absence of women:

> It is obvious what the results of this must be: homosexuality, for instance, and occasional rape cases. But deeper than these there is the degradation worked in man who knows that he is not even considered fit for marriage. The sexual impulse, not to put it any higher, is a fundamental impulse, and starvation of it can be almost as demoralizing as physical hunger (ibid: 116).

The opening paragraph of this new section of 'Such, Such' sets the scene for a lengthy discussion of the sex and homosexuality in particular: '… there was sex, which was always smouldering just under the surface and which suddenly blew up into a tremendous row when I was about twelve' (1952 [1970], 4: 402).

Orwell had actually anticipated the focus on homosexuality with a brief, passing mention of it towards the end of the previous section, confessing that he had 'sneaked' to his favourite teacher Brown 'a suspected case of homosexuality' (ibid: 401). Sex is immediately associated with secrecy, betrayal, ignorance, confusion and shame: 'I did not know very well what homosexuality was, but I knew that it happened and was bad, and that this one of the contexts in which it was proper to sneak. Brown told me I was "a good fellow", which made me feel horribly ashamed' (ibid: 401-402). Now the drama surrounding the 'tremendous row' is narrated. The general outlines are first sketched. Orwell claims he doesn't know precisely what went on, but he imagines it was a group masturbation involving some precocious South American boys (ibid: 402): 'There were summonses, interrogations, confessions, floggings, repentances, solemn lectures of which one understood nothing except some irredeemable sin known as "swinishness" or "beastliness" had been committed' (ibid). All the boys are made to feel implicated.

The spotlight suddenly then falls on Blair. There is mockery and irony when he writes: 'A solemn, black-haired imbecile of an assistant master, who was later to be a member of Parliament [a dig, then, at the political elite] took the older boys to a secluded room and delivered a talk on the Temple of the Body' (ibid: 403). Suddenly, he sets his 'cavernous black eyes' on Blair and adds sadly: '… you I hear are one of the very worst.' His guilt was confirmed and all the terrors surrounding sexuality come to haunt him. 'I too had done the dreadful thing, whatever it was, that wrecked you for life, body and soul, and ended in suicide or the lunatic asylum.'

All this leads Orwell into a remarkably frank account of his own sex life but commenting on the development of sexuality of youths in general when appropriate. Bowker highlights throughout his biography Orwell's predisposition to secrecy: 'While in many ways he could be brutally honest about himself, some aspects of him remained concealed behind a carefully constructed persona, secret sides of himself he seems to have feared and which he may have hoped would remain hidden, even beyond the grave' (op cit: 3). Perhaps the fact that Orwell knew 'Such, Such' was not to be published during his lifetime gave him the psychological space to open up – and perhaps fictionalise, too.

Orwell is often accused of being a misogynist.[6] In fact, Orwell's attitude to women is far more complex. In his handling of his son, Richard, for instance, he was in many ways a New Man, changing nappies (though admittedly with a cigarette in his mouth), showing him real affection and love.[7] Gordon Bowker comments (2003: 48): 'With the exception of an occasional attempt to interpret his dreams, Orwell was never much impressed by psychoanalysis.' But if being open about one's feelings and sexuality (making the personal political) is another mark of today's New Man, then Orwell was well ahead of his times. Here, he admits to being 'in an almost sexless state, which is normal or at any rate common in boys of that age' (ibid). Carefully, he teases out the chronology of his sexual awakening. At five or six, 'like many children' (so deliberately generalising from the personal), he passes through a phase of sexuality.

RICHARD LANCE KEEBLE

> My friends were the plumber's children up the road, and we used sometimes to play games of a vaguely erotic kind. One was called 'playing at doctors' and I remember getting a faint but definitely pleasant thrill from holding a toy trumpet, which was supposed to be a stethoscope, against a little girl's belly (Orwell 1952 [1970, 4: 403).

Again, he draws out the general reflection from the personal anecdote: he falls deeply in love with a girl named Elsie (significantly known only by her first name unlike the boys who are mostly known by their family names) at the convent school he attended: 'She seemed to me grown up, so I suppose she must have been fifteen. After that, as so often happens, all sexual feelings seemed to go out of me for many years' (ibid: 404). Orwell goes on to dwell on his boyhood sexual confusions with what appears to be a compelling honesty, which is all the more challenging for the reader given the deliberate positioning of the essay in the uncertain gap between fact and fiction. Most of the Facts of Life (those first letters capitalised to indicate their Importance and Severity) he learns from observing animals. 'I knew all the dirty words and in my bad moments I would repeat them to myself, but I did not know what the worst of them meant, not want to know. They were abstractly wicked, a sort of verbal charm' (ibid). The paragraph climaxes with him noticing his penis sometimes standing of its own accord, and he comes to believe (or half believe) that the 'crime' that sparked the row was linked to that. 'At any rate, it was something to do with the penis – so much I understood. Many other boys, I have no doubt [that phrase adding extra rhetorical persuasiveness], were equally in the dark' (ibid).

Boys' Own Stories
Having attempted to link his own psychological exploration with the plight of boys in general, Orwell now introduces a 'human interest' element, switching the focus of the narrative to the plight of three boys who are all significantly named: Ronalds, Heath, Beacham and Horne (either pseudonyms to protect identities or all of them mere fictions). The sounds of Ronalds being flogged by Sambo are heard. But Flip's eyes settle on Blair. Confusion and guilt (the dominant feeling of the boy Blair) return. '"You see," she said. I will not swear that she said "You see what you have done," but that was the sense of it. We were all bowed down with shame' (ibid: 405). Heath is forced to read from the Bible: 'Who so shall offend one of these little ones that believe in me, it were better for him that a millstone were hanged about his neck, and that he were drowned in the depth of the sea ' (ibid). Flip taunted Heath who breaks down into 'snivelling tears'. Beacham is 'similarly overwhelmed' after being accused of having black rings round his eyes'. Later, Orwell realises these were supposed to be symptoms by which masturbators could be detected. Without knowing this

at the time, he accepts the black rings are a sign of depravity and gazes anxiously into glass 'looking for the first hint of that dreaded stigma, the confession, which the secret sinner writes upon his own face' (ibid: 406).

In contrast, the final story – about Horne who had been flogged and expelled – brings some light to an otherwise dark narrative. Horne is sent to Eastbourne College, which is despised by Sambo. 'You had no chance if you went to a school like that: at best your destiny would be a clerkship.' But in the following term he meets Horne in the street. He looks normal, not at all ashamed of being at the other college – and glad to have escaped St Cyprian's. But the dark swiftly returns: 'I still believed in the sexual mythology that had been taught me by Sambo and Flip. The mysterious, terrible dangers were still there' (ibid).

SECTION V: CONTRADICTORY CODES

Education into Snobbery

The opening part of this new section moves away from the intense narrative (involving the fates of the four boys) and reflects on broader social, cultural, sporting and class-based issues. The first sentence sets the scene: 'The various codes which were presented to you at St Cyprian's – religious, moral, social and intellectual – contradicted one another if you worked out their implications' (ibid: 407). He highlights the 'sheer vulgar fatness of wealth' in the years before 1914. And adds in a sweeping historical generalisation: 'After 1918 it was never quite the same again. Snobbishness and expensive habits came back, certainly, but they were self-conscious and on the defensive' (ibid: 409). Other intriguing features of the broader cultural scene he considers are the 'curious cult of Scotland' and the values associated with competitive sports.

> Virtue consisted in winning: it consisted in being bigger, stronger, handsomer, richer, more popular, more elegant, more unscrupulous than other people – in dominating them, bullying them, making them suffer pain, making them look foolish, getting the better of them in every way. Life was hierarchical and whatever happened was right (Ibid: 411).

The Instinct to Survive

In keeping with the overall intention in the essay to be 'even-handed' rather than dogmatically polemical, Orwell writes that his sense of guilt and inevitable failure 'was balanced by something else: that is, the instinct to survive' (ibid: 413). This instinct is dramatised in a confrontation with a boy named 'Johnny Hale' (unusual in being given a first name). After Hale picks on him for some reason, Orwell smashes his fist into his face (ibid: 414). How much is this Orwell, the intellectual – and later imperial policeman and Republican militiaman in the Spanish civil war (1936-1937) – still needing to prove his manliness in a conventional aggressive way?

This section ends following the chronological order with Blair/Orwell saying good-bye to Flip. The tension and hatred remain to the very end as does his sensitivity to language, its rhythms and the tone of expression:

> The tone in which she said good-bye was nearly the tone in which she had used to say *little butterflies* [italics in the original]. I had won two scholarships [to Wellington and Eton] but I was a failure, because success was measured not by what you did but by what you were. I was 'not a good type of boy' and could bring no credit on the school (ibid: 416).

SECTION VI: REFLECTIONS
The only certainty is uncertainty

Orwell deliberately mixes the personal and political throughout this final section. First, he sets the scene, then asks a question: 'All this was thirty years ago and more. The question is: Does a child at school go through the same kind of experiences nowadays?' But he is determined to stress the impossibility of knowing. 'The only honest answer, I believe, is that we do not with certainty know' (ibid: 417). His over-emphatic assertiveness in the following sentence, in fact, paradoxically betrays his uncertainty: 'Of course, it is obvious that the present-day attitude towards education is enormously more humane and sensible than that of the past.' Later on he even qualifies that claim: 'The child and the adult live in different worlds. If that is so, we cannot be certain the school, at any rate boarding school, is not still for many children as dreadful an experience as it used to be' (ibid: 421).

CONCLUSION: CONFRONTING HUMBUG

In 'Why I Write', Orwell listed 'four great motives for writing' – putting aside the need to earn a living (1946 [1970, 1: 25-26]): aesthetic enthusiasm, historical impulse, political purpose. But for No 1 motive he said: 'Sheer egoism: Desire to seem clever, to be talked about, to be remembered after death, to get your own back on grown-ups who snubbed you in childhood, etc etc. It is humbug to pretend that this is not a motive and a strong one.' Certainly, in 'Such, Such Were the Joys' Orwell achieved enormous pleasure in crafting the memoir as a deliberately literary piece in the many ways identified in this paper. At the same time, he was certainly getting his own back at Flip and Sambo.

In the essay's final, long paragraph, Orwell looks back in loathing at his time at St Cyprian's. Writing about it has, in any case, been cathartic: 'Now, however, the place is out of my stem for good. Its magic [a strangely positive-sounding word] works no longer, and I have not even enough animosity left to make me hope that Flip and Sambo are dead or that the story of the school being burnt down was true' (ibid: 422).[8] That final word is the crucial one: Orwell wants to leave us wondering: how much do truth and fiction mix in his memoir – as indeed in all history.

NOTES

[1] The exact year when Orwell composed the essay is not known. Crick devotes a whole Appendix in his biography (1980: 586-589) to the topic. He cites Ian Angus who, with Sonia Orwell, edited the *Collected Essays, Journalism and Letters*, who says it 'was written by May 1947' (1970, 4: 330). Crick, in contrast, suggests that 'its uncertain pose between the autobiographical and the polemical, is far more consistent with his bitter and jagged writing of the 1938-43 period, with his mood of failure and frustration, indeed, than with the calm, composed and measured post-war essays' (op cit: 587)

[2] See http://spartacus-educational.com/Jthackeray.htm, accessed on 9 February 2018

[3] See Samuel Butler's *Erewhon*: Dystopia before dystopia, by Oliver Tearle. Available online at https://interestingliterature.com/2018/02/02/samuel-butlers-erewhon-dystopia-before-dystopia/, accessed on 8 February 2018

[4] Ibid

[5] See https://www.the-tls.co.uk/articles/public/locked-up-beyond-reach/, accessed on 9 February 2018

[6] Bowker quotes the poet Stephen Spender (2003: 128): 'Orwell was very misogynist. I don't know why. [He] was a strange sort of eccentric man full of strange ideas and stranger prejudices. One was that he thought that women were extremely inferior and stupid. ... He rather despised women.' See also Patai, Daphne (op cit) and Csaszar, Ivett (2010) Orwell and women's issues: A shadow over the champion of decency, *Eger Journal of English Studies*, Vol. 10 pp 39-56. Available online at http://anglisztika.ektf.hu/new/content/tudomany/ejes/ejesdokumentumok/2010/Csaszar_2010.pdf, accessed on 11 February 2018

[7] See Venables, Dione (n. d) George Orwell: Plain speaking and hidden agendas. Available online at https://www.orwellfoundation.com/the-orwell-foundation/orwell/resources/dione-venables-orwell-plain-speaking-and-hidden-agendas/, accessed on 11 February 2018

[8] The school actually did burn down in 1939: see Taylor, D. J. (op cit: 36)

REFERENCES

Bowker, Gordon (2003) *George Orwell*, London: Little, Brown

Connolly, Cyril (1938 [1961]) *Enemies of Promise*, London: Routledge and Kegan Paul; Harmondsworth, Middlesex: Penguin Books

Crick, Bernard (1980) *George Orwell: A Life*, Harmondsworth, Middlesex: Penguin

CWGO (1989) *The Collected Works of George Orwell*, Vols 1-20, Davison, Peter (ed.) London: Secker and Warburg

Grant, Julia (2004) A real boy and not a sissy: Gender, childhood and masculinity, 1890-1940, *Journal of Social History*, Vol. 37 No. 4 pp 829-851

Keeble, Richard (2007) Introduction: On journalism, creativity and the imagination, Keeble, Richard and Wheeler, Sharon (eds) *The Journalistic Imagination: Literary Journalists from Defoe to Capote and Carter*, London/New York: Routledge pp 1-14

Keeble, Richard Lance (2012) Introduction: Orwell – the cultural icon of today,

RICHARD LANCE KEEBLE

Keeble, Richard Lance (ed.) *Orwell Today*, Bury St Edmunds: Abramis pp 5-12

Lewis, Jeremy (1998) *Cyril Connolly: A Life*, London: Pimlico

Marks, Peter (2011) *George Orwell the Essayist: Literature, Politics and the Periodical Culture*, London/New York: Continuum

Meyers, Jeffrey (2000) *Orwell: Wintry Conscience of a Generation*, New York/London: W. W. Norton & Company

Orwell, George (1931 [1968]) The spike, *Adelphi*, April; Orwell, Sonia and Angus, Ian (eds) *The Collected Essays, Journalism and Letters, Vol. 1: An Age Like This, 1920-1940*, Harmondsworth, Middlesex: Penguin Books pp 58-66

Orwell, George (1933 [1980]) *Down and Out in Paris and London*, *George Orwell*, London: Secker and Warburg/Octopus pp 15-120

Orwell, George (1946 [1970, 1]) Why I Write, Orwell, Sonia and Angus, Ian (eds) *The Collected Essays, Journalism and Letters, Vol. 1: An Age Like This, 1920-1940*, Harmondsworth, Middlesex: Penguin Books pp 23-30

Orwell, George (1952 [1970, 4]) Such, Such Were the Joys, *Partisan Review*, September-October; Orwell, Sonia and Angus, Ian (eds) *The Collected Essays, Journalism and Letters, Vol. 4: In Front of Your Nose 1945-1950*, Harmondsworth, Middlesex: Penguin Books pp 379-422

Patai, Daphne (1984) *The Orwell Mystique: A Study in Male Ideology*, Amherst: University of Massachusetts Press

Sutherland, John (2016) *Orwell's Nose: A Pathological Biography*, London: Reacktion Books

Symonds, John Addington (1968) *The Memoirs of John Addington Symonds*, Grosskurth, Phyllis (ed.) London: Hutchinson

Taylor, D. J. (2003) *Orwell: The Life*, London: Chatto & Windus

Woloch, Alex (2016) *Or Orwell: Writing and Democratic Socialism*, Cambridge, Massachusetts and London: Harvard University Press

NOTE ON THE CONTRIBUTOR

Richard Lance Keeble is Professor of Journalism at the University of Lincoln and Visiting Professor at Liverpool Hope University. His latest book is *Covering Conflict: The Making and Unmaking of New Militarism*, Bury St Edmunds: Abramis 2017.

REVIEWS

Modernism at the Microphone: Radio, Propaganda, and Literary Aesthetics during World War II
Melissa Dinsman
Bloomsbury Academic, London, 2017 pp xiv+250
ISBN 9781350028456 (pbk)

In 1928, Edward Bernays published *Propaganda*, a study of the 'vast and continuous effort going on to capture our minds in the interest of some policy or commodity or idea'. The book addresses both overt information campaigns and the 'unseen mechanism' that manipulates 'the organized habits and opinions of the masses'. Bernays argues that propaganda is an inevitable part of democratic society as proponents for any political cause will try to inform the public about the benefits of their view and the negative aspects of others. But propaganda is, of course, more than just a part of the political process. The freedom of choice provided by capitalist competition in the marketplace means that corporate propaganda presents other examples of this mechanism for manipulation.

The field of 'public relations' emerged around the same time as Bernays's book as corporations – whose advertisements had been longstanding examples of propaganda – now looked into less overt, more 'unseen' means of courting customers. What government and corporate agents were both seeking were ways of shaping public opinion on a range of topics and through diverse tactics. Walter Lippmann's *Public Opinion* (1922) had come out a few years before Bernays's book and put a phrase to the target of campaigns to change minds. Public relations, public opinion and propaganda: these were not just theories in the ether of the 1920s, they were key components of institutions that emerged in Britain during this period. As Britain's first public relations expert Stephen Tallents wrote in 1933, Britain needed to 'master the art of national projection'. And the Empire Marketing Board, the General Post Office, the British Council and the BBC implemented forms of national propaganda that included new technologies, art and literature.

Recent work on the inter-war period has looked into these campaigns, the networks they included and promoted, and their impact on 1930s literature and culture. George Orwell drew attention to the links between literature and propaganda – and literature as propaganda – in his 1941 BBC broadcast 'The Frontiers of Art and Propaganda'. Orwell identifies what he sees as a drastic shift among writers of the 1930s. While the previous generation that included Joyce, Eliot, and Woolf were mainly interested in technique, '30s writers such as Auden, Spender and MacNeice were more attuned to political context and, according to Orwell, 'the most lively criticism' of the time 'looks on every book virtually as a political pamphlet'.

What, then, of 1940s writers – in particular, writers like Orwell hired by the BBC as part of the wartime campaign of national projection? This is the subject of Melissa Dinsman's book *Modernism at the Microphone: Radio, Propaganda, and Literary Aesthetics during World War II*, recently released in paperback by Bloomsbury Academic. Dinsman brings together some fascinating case studies of Orwell, Dorothy L. Sayers and Louis MacNeice – who all broadcast during the war for the BBC – as well as Thomas Mann's and Archibald MacLeish's broadcasts from the US and Ezra Pound's from Italy.

The chapter on Sayers ('Militarizing the Messiah') uses her radio play *The Man Born to be King* (1943) to consider propaganda and religion. MacNeice's chapter focuses on his play *Christopher Columbus* (1944) and wider attempts to forge a closer trans-Atlantic alliance with the US. Archibald MacLeish and Ezra Pound provide examples of what Dinsman calls 'clogged communication', failures to communicate because of difficulties in these writers' works and problems with radio technology. The chapter on Thomas Mann likens him to a ghost haunting his homeland through broadcasts recorded in Los Angeles, shipped to London and transmitted via the BBC to Germany. An Epilogue considers what we might call counter-propaganda through an analysis of P. G. Wodehouse's German broadcasts to the US. These, and the chapter on Orwell – which I discuss in more detail below – spend some time establishing the validity of the book's title, proving that these are, indeed, examples of 'modernism' at the microphone.

In this, the book aligns with the current trend in modernist studies that privileges research framed as a contributor/complicator of the already flexible field of modernism. The other important theoretical framework for the chapters is media/radio studies, particularly with reference to ideas of the network. The introduction offers a useful synthesis of work in this field by, among others, Friedrich Kittler and Marshall McLuhan, and Chapter One provides historical context with detailed research on early radio, Adorno and a close reading of *The Wizard of Oz* (1939). 'Surrender Dorothy', written in the sky by the Wicked Witch of the West, is an example of what Dinsman calls the 'language of the air' – a metaphor for radio transmission and its mobilisation in wartime. This language of the air involved broadcasting the forms of propaganda detailed in the different chapters and the formation of on-air and other networks, both human and machine. It is the examination of the different forms of propaganda (religious, poetry, play, etc.) and the people that produced it that mark the strengths of this book and, in this, the chapter on Orwell and his colleagues working for the BBC Indian Section is exemplary.

Dinsman touches on some potent material: differences between direct and subtle forms of propaganda, text and sub-text, Orwell's ideas about imperialism and the potential of radio, and the idea of literature as propaganda that he brings up in his 1941 broadcast. As Dinsman describes, Orwell did not only see the writers of the '30s as politically motivated (in fact, he cared neither for their writing nor their politics). He found all writing to be political. Dinsman quotes from his essay on Charles Dickens: 'every writer, especially every novelist, *has* a "message", whether he admits it or not, and the minutest details of his work are influenced by it'; in other words: 'All art is propaganda.' Of course, as Orwell went on: 'Not all propaganda is art.' What happens, then, when the writer's message mixes with national propaganda? In Orwell's case, this seems to have been a fruitful match. He was able to work among a diverse group that included T. S. Eliot, Una Marson and Mulk Raj Anand (the famous photograph of the entire group is reprinted here). He also launched *Voice*, an 'on-air literary magazine' that tested the propaganda potential of literature – and the literary potential of propaganda, in this case, propaganda that hoped 'to create a community of Indian students sympathetic to the British war effort', as Dinsman explains.

REVIEW

Other aims, though, could be interpolated into this broader one – even expressions of sympathy for Indian independence. Dinsman makes the case that the voices of *Voice* gave some 'subtle hints' in this direction. Anand comments, in a *Voice* broadcast, that 'war may be necessary, just as a surgical operation may be necessary. Even an operation which may leave you mutilated for life'. Speaking after Anand in the same broadcast, Orwell notes that 'there can be actual enthusiasm for war when it's for some cause such as national liberation'. While he speaks of the French resistance, Dinsman raises the possibility that the Indian audience would have read into these lines support for their own independence. Such is the subtlety of literary propaganda and the difficulties these writers had in communicating clearly their messages.

Close readings like this offer some nuance to the literary propaganda of World War Two, and Dinsman also draws out details about the connections that could be made as a result of these broadcasts: between the broadcasters, between radio presenter and listener, between 'modernist literary aesthetics' and the masses. None of these broadcasts were particularly successful as propaganda. But, as *Modernism at the Microphone* demonstrates, their attempts to inform audiences and shape public opinion can educate us about the politics, aesthetics and unseen mechanisms of the language of the air.

Michael McCluskey,
University of York

London Writing of the 1930s

Anna Cottrell

Edinburgh University Press, Edinburgh, 2017 pp 203

ISBN 9781474425643 (hbk); 9781474425667 (PDF); 9781474425650 (pbk); 978147442567 4 (ePub)

This book could have carried a subtitle: 'photographic fictions.' Rather than trying to cover all of the literary writing concerned with contemporary London produced during the 1930s, Cottrell examines a single strand: a new sort of literary naturalism, descended from Zola but altered by technological innovations such as the cinema and the portable camera. This new naturalism, suited to the aims of 1930s documentary fiction, bears more similarities to surrealism and even to abstract visual art than to nineteenth-century realism (pp 6-9; 19-21). In it, female characters are presented as being at once liberated from earlier restraints on where they could live and with whom they could associate, but also as guilty of what Cottrell calls 'thoughtless perception' (p. 4). They – and many of the men who are their companions in this fiction – typically seem frightened, frozen, threatened and isolated in city settings. The key writers are Storm Jameson, Patrick Hamilton, Norah Hoult, Jean Rhys and, slightly less prominently, several others including George Orwell.

Alongside widely admired writers such as Rhys and Orwell, Cottrell takes seriously a sort of writing often dismissed at the time: that characterised by 'skill in rendering subjectivities' using 'meticulously observed external detail'. Cottrell's project develops from the work of new modernism studies expanding the canon of writers considered worth discussing among the multitude who were active in the 1930s. Specifically, this means turning away from the idea that if the 1920s was formally experimental, the 1930s was realist and political, an idea encapsulated in the earlier view of the decades as that of the 'Auden Generation'.

Five chapters follow a thoughtful and accessible introduction. They are structured around two types of spatial category. First, in Chapters 1 and 2, comes the topographic, in which the atmospheres and associations of different city districts are distinguished. Then, in Chapters 3, 4 and 5, follows an analysis of the spatial categories occupied and thematised by Cottrell's chosen writers. Chapter 1 focuses on the West End of London, defined here as the capital's prime entertainment district, within it 'London's brightest street lights, the largest concentration of electric advertising, the most lavish restaurants and cinemas, and the biggest crowds' (p. 35). Chapter 2 contrasts this zone with 'nearby Soho ... where the lights were dimmer, streets narrower, and life seemingly protected from the fake glossiness of the life "Up West"' for writers such as Hamilton who sought 'authenticity' there (p. 59). Chapters 3 and 4 examine public or semi-public spaces, namely the enlarged commercial cafés and cinemas which drew people to central London in the decades after the First World War. Chapter 5's focus is on a sort of domesticity: that of the rented room in the inner city, a favoured type of accommodation among both aspiring writers and the protagonists of their post-naturalist fiction. The first and last chapters, 'Out on the Town' 'Staying Home', moreover, are also paired: both as 'out' versus 'in', and by their shared interest in perception of street images. The latter are typically seen here from a static position resembling a photographer's, whether from the window of a rented room or from a position in a prominent part of the capital such as Piccadilly Circus. Noting continuities with earlier writers' revulsion faced with city crowds (p. 36), Cottrell distinguishes this newly static perspective from 'the pleasures of leisurely streetwalking' (p. 13), presumably as represented by nineteenth-century urban writing.

The book's clear focus on the perceptual qualities recorded in this group of 1930s London fictions brings forth vivid details. These provide flashes of insight into different histories: literary, urban, sensory. Storm Jameson reflected later on her own 'devil of an idea' in the 1930s 'to set myself up as a Balzac' (p. 47). Her projected *roman fleuve* began in 1934 with *Company Parade* within which, Cottrell puts it (p. 46), much is made 'of the fact that London street culture died with the [First World] war, to be resurrected as disingenuous performance'. Herein lies a research question for a future student. If London streets seemed bizarrely quiet after the First World War to people who had been there before, why was that? Was it because the poor had been decanted elsewhere or (the men at least) simply killed? Or had the flowers just disappeared from Covent Garden market, driving the flower girls of old away?

Human bodies and their surroundings appear differently in different lighting conditions, and some of Cottrell's most interesting observations develop from the impact on literature of this material fact (pp 23-24, 37). Discussing Jameson's *A Day Off* (1933), Cottrell observes how its ageing protagonist, in a brightly lit modern teashop, 'becomes immersed in the geometric patterns formed by light on the glittering surfaces' (p. 112). The naturalism that most interests Cottrell pays a grotesque 'hyper-attentiveness to swollen veins and wrinkles', exposed by such lighting, so providing 'an escape route from the Realist mode of writing the city' (pp 112-113). As these points indicate, the book is driven by a powerful sense of visuality, a sensory and ultimately physical quality absent from earlier views of the literary landscape of the 'Thirties' as fundamentally intellectual and ideological in a pattern laid down by Eliot and Auden. Thus, Cottrell defends the 'photographic framing' of a tableau as literary device (pp 10; 9-13) and makes a valuable excursus into the history of technology, examining the materiality of lighting in the West End. She elegantly integrates literary readings with interpretations of photography, notably shots of London, by Bill Brandt, and of Paris, by Brassaï (pp 57-59, 83-84, 120-122).

Orwell himself appears here largely via *Keep the Aspidistra Flying* (pp 43-45, 155-157) and through his qualified rejection of literary naturalism as a preferred mode for his writing at around the time that novel appeared (1936). Surprisingly, Cottrell has little to say about *A Clergyman's Daughter* (1935 [1998]), with its confused, displaced middle-class female protagonist adrift in Depression-era central London. In *A Clergyman's Daughter*, Orwell seems concerned with the grimy rather than the shiny, and it is the shinier aspects of London, however bleak and disturbing, that catch Cottrell's eye. Moreover, George Gissing's importance in the shaping of Orwell's naturalism (and twentieth-century London naturalism generally) is underplayed. This importance should be clear from the claim in the 1943 Orwell essay 'Not Enough Money' that Gissing is 'perhaps the finest novelist England has produced' (Orwell 1943 [1998b: 45]). Dorothy, in *A Clergyman's Daughter*, during her temporary escape from the drudgeries and financial pettifogging of her father's house, spends Christmas Day in a wood near London, having 'her Christmas dinner – a hard-boiled egg, two cheese sandwiches, and a bottle of lemonade … against a great gnarled beech tree, over a copy of George Gissing's *The Odd Women*' (Orwell 1935 [1998a: 256]).

The book's 'London writing' is not writing by Londoners. Hoult was raised in Ireland, Rhys in the Caribbean, Jameson in Yorkshire and at sea. Orwell and Hamilton were public-school men raised in southern England outside London. Writers of the Jewish East End or London specialists from an earlier generation like Thomas Burke are largely absent from Cottrell's account. Post-war Londoner writers like David Lodge frequently continue patterns earlier detectable in 1930s predecessors such as Simon Blumenfeld, in which the famous centre is seen in a relationship, often of contrast admittedly, with a particular quarter of residential or industrial London. Such an imaginative map differs from the expanses of meaningless obscurity typically placed around central London by Rhys and early Orwell. Cottrell (p. 44) observes that Gordon Comstock, in *Keep the Aspidistra Flying*, has a 'tourist' approach to London in which, if he cannot conquer literary society, he will seek 'the simplicity of slum life'. Gordon ends the novel a suburbanite, in a naturalist turn of a non-tragic sort (p. 156). Orwell and Rhys may lodge in London and write of it, but they never present it as an all-encompassing environment, a seemingly complete world.

Such a sense is characteristic of writing by Londoner novelists such as Blumenfeld (himself the child of recent immigrants), as well as of incomers during adulthood such as William Plomer (*The Case Is Altered*, 1932; *The Invaders*, 1934), Nigel Balchin (*The Small Back Room*, 1943) and even Samuel Beckett (*Murphy*, 1938). The tonality of ordinary London backstreet life found in non-fiction writers of social survey and investigative journalism such as Ada Jones Chesterton (*I Lived in a Slum*, 1936) and Marie Paneth (*Branch Street*, 1944) is not absent from Cottrell's book. But it appears only in the context of the central areas, notably Soho, in which writers would happily rent rooms to be close to the heart of things. For Cottrell, Jameson's 1938 novel *Here Comes a Candle*, in which an educated woman marries a carpenter and lives with him in Soho, reveals 'the provincial prejudices that are preserved in pockets of the metropolis that are neglected and unprogressive' (p. 179). The 'neglected' parts of London (Soho cannot be included among them, since writers thematised it so eagerly) remain neglected in Cottrell's book, however.

If Cottrell's writers do not offer only a touristic view of the city, theirs is largely a newcomer's one, focused on the most brightly lit and prominent areas. The topographic distinctions found here do not resemble those of the Londoner. Jerry White (2008: 328) identifies Soho as the 'most bohemian, stimulating, intimate part' of the West End of London, 'firmly established as such by 1900'. For White, in pre-1914 London, 'the great centre of night life and enjoyment was, of course, the West End'. For Cottrell, quite differently, Soho is not a part of the West End but contrasts with it (since she defines the West End as the most brightly lit portion of the municipal City of Westminster, that of Piccadilly Circus and Leicester Square, the zone of the biggest cafés and cinemas). She argues that the West End as mass entertainment zone was largely a post-1914 phenomenon and that her writers' interest in its nocturnal aspect was also novel, their 'nineteenth-century equivalents' having covered 'mainly … the East End and its picturesque landscapes of poverty and vice' (p. 65).

REVIEW

But the West End had been at the heart of fictions of both high society and vicious lowlife since at least the end of the eighteenth century, for instance in the pre-Victorian and early Victorian writings of Thackeray, Bulwer-Lytton and Pierce Egan. And when literary authors such as Walter Besant proposed in the 1880s to introduce readers to the East End they often deployed the trope of being *In Darkest London*, as Margaret Harkness's *Captain Lobe: A Story of the Salvation Army* was renamed in 1890 (Janssen 2014; Ross 2007: 89-91), as part of a claim that the area they wrote about was hitherto unexplored.

Cottrell works in tandem with assertions of a 'long 1930s' (Mellor and Salton-Cox 2015) succeeding the earlier categorisations of Bernard Bergonzi, Samuel Hynes and Valentine Cunningham, who risked reducing the decade's story to writing by politically committed male writers with Oxbridge and BBC connections. Cottrell's historicism moves between close-up views of 1930s moments and a more panoramic perspective on literary views of urbanity from Zola to Barthes. Still, her 1930s feel tonally similar to the landscape surveyed in Bergonzi's *Reading the Thirties* (1978), published nearly forty years earlier. Both books make the climate of the times seem chilly, even glacial.

Within new modernism studies, Charles M. Tung (2016) has indicated how temporalities that are multiple, potentially clashing and of radically different magnitudes could be integrated with work on handfuls of years. Inspired by Tung, a reading of how multiple histories interact sometimes through relations of influence and long-term tendencies, sometimes through random encounters, would enable contexts largely absent from Cottrell's study to enter view. Among these contexts are the specifics of publishing and marketing, for instance (see Nash 2011), or the specific socio-economic factors surrounding rooms offered for rent in London.

Cottrell certainly makes the case for a deeper engagement with writers such as Jameson and Hoult than the canons of 1930s writing earlier allowed. She persuades me that further exploration is needed of intriguing yet obscure texts such as John Pudney's 1938 Soho novel *Jacobson's Ladder* (pp 88-90). More valuable still could prove her integration of the specific material conditions of pre-World War Two cities, notably the uneven distribution of powerful lighting after dark. A fuller imaginative mapping of 1930s London could follow, building on Cottrell.

REFERENCES

Bergonzi, Bernard (1978) *Reading the Thirties*, London: Macmillan

Janssen, Flore (2014) Margaret Harkness: *In Darkest London* – 1889, *London Fictions*. Available online at www.londonfictions.com/margaret-harkness-in-darkest-london.html, accessed on 16 January 2018

Mellor, Leo and Salton-Cox, Glyn (2015) Introduction, *Critical Quarterly*, Vol. 57, No.3 (Special Issue: 'The Long 1930s') pp 3-19

Nash, Andrew (2011) The production of the novel, Parrinder, Patrick, and Gasiorek, Andrzej (eds) *The Oxford History of the Novel in English, Vol. 4: 1880-1940*, Oxford: Oxford University Press pp 3-19

Orwell, George (1935 [1998a]) *A Clergyman's Daughter*, Davison, Peter (ed.) *Complete Works of George Orwell: Vol. 3*, London: Secker & Warburg

Orwell, George (1943 [1998b]) 'Not enough money': A sketch of George Gissing, *Tribune*, 2 April; Davison, Peter, (ed.) *The Complete Works of George Orwell: Vol. 15*, London: Secker & Warburg pp 45-47

Ross, Ellen (ed.) (2007) *Slum Travellers: Ladies and London Poverty, 1860-1920*, Berkeley: University of California Press

Tung, Charles M. (2016) Baddest Modernism: The scales and lines of inhuman time, *Modernism/modernity*, Vol. 23, No. 3 pp 515-38

White, Jerry (2008) *London in the Twentieth Century: A City and Its People*, London: Vintage

Jason Finch,
Åbo Akademi University

REVIEW

Modern Print Artefacts: Textual Materiality and British Literary Value in British Print Culture, 1890s-1930s

Patrick Collier

Edinburgh University Press, Edinburgh, 2016 pp viii+288

ISBN 9781474413473

John O'London's Weekly had a struggle on its hands. The editors were determined to argue that Joseph Conrad was the era's standout novelist and that *Suspense* (1923), in particular, was a 'novel of absolute genius', whereas their readers tended to disagree (p. 122). Taking arms against a sea of reprints – the magazine serialised *Victory* in 1926 – one anonymous reader wrote to the editors to acknowledge his own and others' 'manful ...' efforts to appreciate the author, while insisting upon a general failure 'to see wherein he was great' (p. 123). It seemed, in fact, that Conrad was 'tedious', unless they were all missing something, since 'they simply could not make heads or tails of him' (ibid).

This was 1926. A couple of decades later, Orwell faced a similar struggle to save Conrad's reputation from the dust pile after his death. He wrote an influential essay about him, urged publishers to reprint *The Secret Agent* (1907), and at his death was planning to write Conrad's biography. Conrad, it seemed to him, 'had a remarkable understanding of the atmosphere of revolutionary movements – an understanding which very few Englishmen would have, and certainly no Englishmen with anything resembling Conrad's political outlook' (Davison 2013: 267). Conrad was a fossil of latent knowledge, so that to ignore him was a kind of philistinism with regard to the past. Would Orwell have convinced the readers of *John O'London's Weekly* to return conscientiously to their mounds of Conrad reprints? Who knows. But one of the great achievements of Patrick Collier's brilliant monograph, *Modern Print Artefacts*, is its ability to show that the construction of literary value required both sorts of promotion: Conrad appears to have been *as* reliant on Orwell's nuanced critical estimation of him as he was on the lively and contingent debate between the editors of *John O'London's Weekly* and their readers, in laying claim to his laurel crown.

Wittgenstein once wrote that taste – when discerning – was a product of honest thinking (McGuiness 2012: 4). And Collier's book may be read as an account of the means by which readers of the *Illustrated London News*, *John O'London's Weekly*, *The Mercury* and a range of prominent poetry anthologies, thought honestly and aloud about late-nineteenth and early-twentieth-century literature. This, of course, was the era of modernism, when conceptualisations of literary value were fundamental to what Lawrence Rainey (1998) has called 'institutions of modernism' – the elaborate network of magazines, publishing houses, editors, writers and readers whose tastes determined what 'modernism' meant to its practitioners and consumers. However, for Collier, Rainey's familiar story of modernism's evolution from a sequence of experiments into a cultural industry risks justifying the elitism of its gatekeepers – from T. S. Eliot in the 1920s to ourselves in the present.

Collier sets out in the postscript of his book – provocatively entitled 'Against "Modernist Studies"' – to undermine the elitist premise of current critical work on modernist literature. His book is a testament to the richness and promise of his own non-modernist angle; and his subject matter has the ethical advantage of modelling a 'democratisation' of critical judgement (p. 154). Nonetheless, it remains unclear to me that the discovery of new fields of inquiry within the late-nineteenth and early-twentieth century print culture should necessarily entail the jettisoning of modernist studies, bearing in mind that the elitist basis of modernism's canon is no longer a blind spot within the historical narrative of this period, but a site of increased knowingness, enlightenment and critique. Why should not Collier's 'democratised' readers coexist happily – or fractiously – with modernism's snobs in the critical arena?

Collier directs his gripe against modernist studies at the attitude expressed by Charles Altieri in an article for *Textual Practice* (2012) that critics should 'track … the contours of the best thinking in the period' (p. 235). For Collier, there is enough toxicity in this snobbish phrase 'best thinking' to render modernist studies defunct. However, if we read Collier's monograph as a meditation on the contingencies of literary taste in the context of modern print culture, then our own critical taste must be seen as contingent in historically rooted ways too, and thus incapable of being wiped away by an anti-modernist purge. Whether or not it is snobbery that persuades some critics (including myself) to research Conrad rather than Hugh Walpole's commentary on Conrad in *John O'London's Weekly* or to seek out back issues of niche modernist magazines rather than those of popular magazines, our preference may not be gainsaid, for although it may not be true that there is no accounting for taste, there is at least no arguing with it.

REFERENCES

Altieri, Charles (2012) Afterword: How the 'New Modernist Studies' fails the Old Modernism, *Textual Practice*, Vol. 26, No. 4 pp 763-782

Davison, Peter (ed.) (2013) *George Orwell: A Life in Letters*, New York: Liveright Publishing

McGuiness, Brian (ed.) (2012) *Wittgenstein in Cambridge: Letters and Documents, 1911-1951*, Chichester: Blackwell

Rainey, Lawrence (1998) *Institutions of Modernism: Literary Elites and Public Culture*, New Haven, Connecticut: Yale University Press

Beci Carver,
University of Exeter

George Orwell

Subscription information
Each volume contains two issues, published half-yearly.

Annual Subscription (including postage)

Personal Subscription

UK	£25
Europe	£28
RoW	£30

Institutional Subscription

UK	£100
Europe	£115
RoW	£120

Single Issue copies (subject to availability)

UK	£15
Europe	£17
RoW	£20

Enquiries regarding subscriptions and orders should be sent to:

> Journals Fulfilment Department
> Abramis Academic
> ASK House
> Northgate Avenue
> Bury St Edmunds
> Suffolk, IP32 6BB
> UK

Tel: +44(0)1284 700321
Email: info@abramis.co.uk

www.ingramcontent.com/pod-product-compliance
Lightning Source LLC
Chambersburg PA
CBHW080406170426
43193CB00016B/2830